P9-DGS-433

THE REMOVERS

A Memoir

ANDREW MEREDITH

SCRIBNER

NEW YORK LONDON TORONTO SYDNEY NEW DELHI

Scribner
A Division of Simon & Schuster, Inc.
1230 Avenue of the Americas
New York, NY 10020

Copyright © 2014 by Andrew Meredith

All rights reserved, including the right to reproduce this book or portions thereof in any form whatsoever. For information, address Scribner Subsidiary Rights Department, 1230 Avenue of the Americas, New York, NY 10020.

First Scribner hardcover edition July 2014

SCRIBNER and design are registered trademarks of The Gale Group, Inc., used under license by Simon & Schuster, Inc., the publisher of this work.

For information about special discounts for bulk purchases, please contact Simon & Schuster Special Sales at 1-866-506-1949 or business@simonandschuster.com.

The Simon & Schuster Speakers Bureau can bring authors to your live event. For more information or to book an event, contact the Simon & Schuster Speakers Bureau at 1-866-248-3049 or visit our website at www.simonspeakers.com.

Interior design by Jill Putorti
Jacket design by Evan Gaffney
Jacket photograph © Walter B. McKenzie/The Image Bank/Getty Images

Manufactured in the United States of America

10   9   8   7   6   5   4   3   2   1

Library of Congress Control Number: 2013045780

ISBN 978-1-4767-6121-3
ISBN 978-1-4767-6124-4 (ebook)

Certain names and identifying characteristics have been changed.

To John Klein

Love is not love
which alters when it alteration finds,
or bends with the remover to remove.
—W. S.

We all inherit death, Andrew, but not death alone.
I give dogwoods in the sun to you, who cling like life to bone.
—W. M.

THE
REMOVERS

1

Dad parks the hearse at the curb under a pink-petaled dogwood, in the glory of that first balmy April Saturday afternoon. We're on Castor Avenue in front of a tan brick apartment building, treeless courtyard, three stories high, a block long but invisible, a place that marks the edge of our Philadelphia neighborhood and the next, a structure populated by pensioner bachelor mailmen and mothers and toddlers learning English together. At the rec center baseball diamond across the street, screams of "Go!" follow an aluminum plink. At the corner, tulips in yellow, red, violet, planted to partition the sidewalk from a tiny row house lawn, salute a crew-cut man in a tank top, gold crucifix swinging as he soapy-sponges his four-wheeled stereo. The fried onions from the grill at the steak shop a block away whisper that the cold and dark have passed and we've been delivered somewhere better, and yet inside our little brick houses these last six months a secret part of us wondered: is this the year winter doesn't end? A girthy old woman in her sleeveless summer housedress, sunlight warming her arms for the first time this year, hoses the dirt under her rosebush. She looks like a Helen. She might be a Carol. An ambulance lines up at the red light like all the other cars, in repose, maybe coming back from an oil change.

Dad and I leave the car and walk into the courtyard where a man in a fishing hat and a yellowed V-neck T-shirt, maybe sixty-five, sucking a cigarette, raises a hand. "I'm the brother-in-law," he says. It's sunny, humid. Dad is fifty years old, solidly built, clean-shaven, glasses, gray hair shiny and wavy like a trial lawyer's. He cuts his own hair in the bathroom mirror because he knows he can do better than any barber left in our neighborhood. I am a head taller than he, gangly, a day past clean-shaven, with glasses, and, though not balding or a mental patient, I keep my hair in a self-inflicted buzz mostly because I assume I would screw up a scissor cut. If the brother-in-law had met us in different circumstances, when he wasn't in shock, he might've noticed the same long nose on both of these removers. Or at least he would've noticed the sweat beading on our foreheads. Or my polyester suit: a fledgling. Or how sharp Dad looks—suit of lightweight wool, loafers polished and tassled, white pocket square, as if he'd slid dressed like this out of the womb. But the brother-in-law doesn't really see us. He says hello, of course, and thanks us for coming, but the living parts of him have retreated far away behind the corneas. I recognize this kind of distance.

Besides, the brother-in-law has never seen us before and will never want to again, these who've shown up on what I guess is the worst day he's had in a while. Maybe ever. We are nobodies. Strangers. We aren't the funeral director who perches every Sunday in the front pew at mass. We are men made to be forgotten, here to take away the shell of his brother-in-law. He'll never think on us again. I feel right away a rush from this. We're paid to be invisible. And yet there's another part of me—reasonable, accountable, button-down—that likes how useful this work makes me. The brother-in-law says, "Carl lived alone. We hadn't heard from him for a few weeks, which wasn't strange, but the neighbors called the cops today about a smell." He opens his eyes a little wider and shakes his head. "He's been in there awhile."

Just as I had dismissed my dad's assurances on my first removal, I brush aside the brother-in-law's warning. He's not used to these things the way we are, I think. I assume I've seen and touched and smelled the limits of the job's gruesomeness. By the time we've walked the few paces to Carl's front door, I know I'm wrong again. His windows and the door are shut, but what awaits us seeps out. At the first whiff my heart feels like it might come bursting through my armpit. Dad looks at me and says, "We'll be okay." When he opens Carl's front door I have never smelled anything worse—imagine being waterboarded on the hottest day of summer with the maggoty brine dripping from the back of a garbage truck—and we're still fifteen feet from the closed bedroom. We move to the back of the apartment, wheeling the stretcher, breathing through our jacket sleeves. We stop just outside his room. Dad and I don't speak, but share a look. I know, in my eyes at least, there's terror. How bad will it be in there? What will this guy look like? But there's also an element of disbelief: Have our lives really brought us here? Is Dad the guy with a book of poems? Am I the kid who won a full ride to college a few years ago? A split second where the job's simple awfulness brings into focus the downward trajectory of our circumstance.

———

When I was old enough to know the kind of place we lived in—blocks and blocks of brick row houses dotted occasionally with a brick factory or a stone church, and cut through by train tracks and highways—one of my favorite things Dad would do was drive the two of us along Snake Road, a stretch he called "the country in the city." Only a mile from our house, Snake Road runs through woods, the only such break in our part of town. Every few months in these first years of my awareness of the world, he would wind us through the trees. Every time, as we came back into the grid of the neighborhood, it felt to me for a finger snap of a moment that we belonged to that wilderness more than we did to our house, and belonged to each other more than we did to my mother and sister inside it.

———

It's time to open the bedroom door. Never before have I felt anything as dreadful as what hits us when we enter. The windows are closed—his last night, probably at least a week before, must have been a cold one—so the stench surges at us like a crashing wave, coating our faces and rushing into our nostrils and mouths. My stomach closes like a fist, shoulders jump toward ears. My scalp tingles. The odor is an exponentially more putrid relative of late afternoon low tide, when the summer sun has spent a full day cooking the rotten gunk on the bay floor. But that is an inadequate comparison. In the context of a stale, dilapidated apartment building, Carl's stink screams an urgent and violent disharmony. We smell death.

Lying on his back, Carl looks like any napping retiree, except he's purple. And gravity has pulled almost all the liquid in his body into his lower hemisphere—his back and ass and the backs of his legs—which makes him a head to toe bedsore, a seeping blister ready to gush. As awful as it is to look at Carl and smell him, being that close to him somehow shoos away any fear or hesitation. Pity fills the void. He's just a poor soul who happens to be rotting in his bed. And it's difficult, I'm finding, to handle an older man's corpse with your father—a man, odds say, you will one day bury—and avoid thinking of your father's death. And when the older man you're removing lives alone in your neighborhood, and your father and your mother don't get along, and you expect they could be living separately any day now, it's hard not to imagine your father dying like this, in an anonymous building in Frankford, going rotten like a pack of chicken breasts forgotten in the trunk, and you playing the brother-in-law's role, you letting yourself in and wading through the death smell to see him melting into his mattress. It's strange, maybe inappropriate, to include my fifty-year-old father in a thought like this, but I wonder if the two of us will make something of ourselves before that day arrives.

We know we can't or, rather, don't want to breathe near Carl, so we decide to work in breath-long shifts—one guy in the bedroom at a time—like kids in the deep end of a pool trying to grab a quarter off the bottom. But this strategy can only last so long. Lifting the body in its bedsheet, the norm for in-bed removals, is out of the question for Carl. If we hoist him like that, the pressure of his weight against the sheet will split him like an overripe peach, with fluids rushing through the fabric, leaving a mess we don't want to witness or clean up. Instead we'll have to fasten him to the plastic sheet we've brought along, a tool called the Reeves.

Lined with narrow boards, the Reeves is firmer than a bedsheet, and so offers a better distribution of support of the body when lifted, and since it's plastic, no leaks. The drawback, though: using the Reeves requires not a small amount of handling the deceased. The man who taught me to throw a baseball now stands on the right side of the bed and reaches across for Carl's left arm and left leg. "Like this," he says through a grimace. When he pulls the limbs up off the mattress, I shimmy the Reeves under as far as I can. Then we switch. In Carl's case, lifting him means loosing all the stink caught between him and the bed. It also means gripping his flesh, which, through rubber gloves, feels like squeezing a Ziploc bag filled with tomato sauce. We work like a pair of gymnast surgeons, summoning a precise mix of speed and delicacy that I have never imagined within our genetic grasps. In a few minutes the three of us are outside in the fresh air of the courtyard. The brother-in-law has disappeared.

The ride to the funeral home is its own horror, especially at red lights, when the air stops moving. But breathing in the open-windowed car with the AC roaring doesn't compare to breathing in Carl's coffin of a bedroom. Unloading him from the Reeves onto the embalming table in the air-conditioned funeral home morgue is also a diminished echo of its mirror act. And then we go home and life is normal. I eat a fore-arm-size Italian hoagie leaky with oil and tomato drippings, without thinking of Carl's seepage. I talk to my mother in the kitchen and watch her go silent and stiff in the shoulders when my father comes in. I go to Gazz's apartment that night and we pound Miller Lite while his girlfriend and his baby sleep in the other room and we watch the Sixers on mute and he drags out his boom box and puts on "Couldn't You Wait?" by Silk-worm and then I play Todd Rundgren's "We Gotta Get You a Woman" and he chooses "Dry Your Eyes" by Brenda and the Tabulations and then we play "Bobby Jean" and Bruce—Bruce, our beloved uncle (long lost, made good); Bruce, on our parents' stereos since the crib; Bruce, patron saint of Philly white boys' first sips of disappointment; Bruce, no last name required or ever, ever used—tells us *we liked the same music we liked the same bands we liked the same clothes*, and so begins another night of *telling each other we were the wildest* and pull-ing one gem after another from Gazz's laundry basket loaded with CDs and cassettes.

Hours later I drive home drunk up Tulip Street hollering along to Pavement's "Fillmore Jive." "*I need to sleep it off,*" I sing. When it ends I rewind and do it again. I'm only a few weeks into this funeral business and already I'm feeling that a certain gift of mine—becoming okay with anything that happens even as I am powerless to change it—is being put to the best use possible. There are all sorts of careers that need active, aggressive personalities, but not this one. The remover affects a normal life and then the little plastic matchbox in his pocket vibrates and he goes and puts on his black suit and in half an hour he's pulling your dead ass out of bed with his knees, not his back. The dead body picker-upper, he accepts what life brings. He's not out evangelizing for salad greens and thirty minutes of cardio. He's not caught up fighting the unfightable. He doesn't turn his anxiety into fake-hustle like a New Yorker. He accepts. He's a model phlegmatic, like William Penn. He is a Philadelphian by nature. You're dead and you need a lift.

A month before my father and I picked up Carl, I was unemployed. I was twenty-two. I lived with my parents, who hadn't spoken to each other for eight years, in Northeast Philadelphia, in a neighborhood called Frankford, in the row house I grew up in. On this night I was doing my usual thing of standing on the front steps after everyone had gone to bed, getting buzzed on a string of Camel unfiltereds. I waited for my parents to go upstairs because I didn't want my mother to know I smoked. My younger sister, Theresa, my only sibling, was living across town in a dorm at the University of Pennsylvania. Alone out there on the top step I became the star of my own movie, in my shearling coat, smoking my Camels, flicking away the butts, greeting passing cars with squinty tough-guy looks, though it was too dark for them to see my face. I liked to smoke six or seven in a row to feel light-headed, to feel different than I did in the house, to stain my fingers yellow. On this night I brought my Walkman out so I could listen, again, to Pavement's *Crooked Rain, Crooked Rain*. I was looking for something in that album, some clue to myself that could be illuminated by the feeling its songs gave me—a sense of spiritual soaring. How could they grant me such lightness, I wondered, when every other minute of the day felt like lead?

Every fifteen minutes or so a bus pulled up at the corner. How odd for a lit room of strangers to appear out of the dark, stop, roll away. The J, the K, and the 75 all stop at Oakland and Orthodox. Each route starts in Frankford, the place where I had always lived, where my parents had lived almost their whole lives, where my parents' parents had lived, where my mother's grandparents and great-grandparents lived back to when these blocks were farms. And these three routes all connect Frankford to the northwest part of the city: Logan, Germantown, Olney. Olney's where I had ridden these buses to most often. As a toddler sometimes I would ride the bus with my father to La Salle College, where he taught English and from which he'd graduated in the early seventies. And up until two years previously, I rode the bus there to go to class at La Salle myself. But I dropped out in the middle of my junior year. Not a huge failure, then again it wasn't the flunking out that worried me. I used to be smart. Used to be funny. Now I was the kid who waited for everyone to go to sleep so I could smoke. I'm not a smoker. Now I was the Silent Kid, and Pavement's singer, Stephen Malkmus, was the one person who knew how to talk to me. "*Silent kid . . . let's talk about leaving,*" he says. "*Come on, now. Talk about your family.*" I don't want to talk about my family, Malkmus. I practiced unsophisticated astronomy through the light pollution of streetlamps. Orion! I rarely ventured off the top step. I could have gone for a walk around the block or even up and down the street, but I didn't want to risk it. There could be possums. Periodically I scraped my sneakers on the concrete to spook anything nocturnal that might've been creeping in the hedges. Also, I didn't want to get jumped. I didn't risk much in the daytime either. The sweep of my ambition was confined to dubbing mix tapes for Gazz and hunting in Salvation Armies and Goodwills for secondhand T-shirts I could see Malkmus wearing. The voice in my head that told me this was all wrong, that days and nights like this were sins against myself, I did my best to drown out with Pavement and sports talk radio. I was dreadful broke.

The day before this night on the step, I worked up the courage to ask my father if I could get a job at the place he worked part-time. It didn't sound too hard. I had a driver's license. I wasn't physically disabled. There may have been some questions about whether I was a good fit for this kind of work, but I'd reached financial crisis. I had no choice.

My father's bedroom door was open and he was lying on his bed in the dark wearing headphones, listening to his Irish music. I stood there until he pulled one side away from his ear.

I said, "Do you think I could work for Livery of Frankford?"

He said, "I'll ask."

I said, "Thanks." That was a big conversation for us.

Then I went back to my room to finish dubbing Gazz a mix, the format of which was an alternating pattern of what I'd decided were the greatest hits of the Silver Jews and the Shirelles. The next afternoon Dad came home from his other job as a college English teacher in Camden and dropped a paper bag in my lap. "I got it at Salvation Army," he said. Inside was a black polyester suit that smelled of trapped sweat. "Try it on."

People ask how I got into the funeral business, the underlying implication seeming to be, Why would you possibly choose it? The answer is that I had not yet developed any choosing skills. I was a broke dummy just as startled as anyone else to find myself picking up bodies. That was it. And without any sort of vision for myself, I took the job that came my way from someone I knew. That's how everybody I knew got their jobs. They knew somebody who got them in. I could've just as easily become a guy who fixed ice cream freezers in corner stores, the way Gazz did. Guys he knew did that work and got him the job. Choosing didn't seem to have much to do with it.

———————

The next night, a Friday, I was horizontal on the couch in the living room taking in a first-run *Boy Meets World* when the phone rang. Dad answered it in the kitchen, and when I realized it was a work call I hit Mute. I heard him click a ballpoint pen, then repeat an address. When he hung up he called in to me, "Andy, you want to go on a removal?" "Yeah, sure," I said. Nobody in the world wants to go on a removal. The real question is, do you want to make a little money? To which my honest answer would've been, "Eh. Whatever. I guess." But I needed a job to justify all the time I spent in my room with my stereo on. I needed money to pay my phone bill so I could keep calling Gazz every night and playing songs back and forth over the four miles of telephone line between our bedrooms.

I went upstairs to my room and put on my new uniform: white oxford shirt from Salvation Army, an eighth of an inch too small at the neck so that I choked when I looked down; black clip-on tie; black, double-knit Botany 500 suit, the jacket of which had arms that hit just past my gangly wrists but was four inches too big in the chest; pants with a hole along the crotch seam and generous enough at the waist that I gathered the excess fabric in front of me, folded it over, and cinched it under a long black belt, creating the effect of double-breasted pants; and a pair of old brown boots that I'd smeared, in anticipation of my first removal, with black shoe polish. I was the special-needs Reservoir Dog. I was the lowest-ranking agent in the Latvian Secret Service assigned to walk the travel minister's cats. Beneath my suit I wore an aquamarine T-shirt with Greek characters across the chest. The summer I graduated from high school, my dad's friend CJ had given me this shirt with a tag attached explaining that the text was that of the Delphi Oracle: "Know thyself." It went into my regular rotation. I valued the Greek letters' inscrutability. After a few armpit holes, I'd retired it to the back of a drawer. It lay there untouched for a few years before I grabbed it that night to wear under my removal suit. It was perfect. In the mirror I saw the Delphic Clark Kent. I knew nothing about myself.

A brick building in the middle of a block of Fillmore Street row homes. You could have driven down this dreary, treeless stretch every day of your life and not noticed the livery garage. Not taller than the neighboring homes. Made of the same muted brick. And yet inside was enough room for a half dozen silver limousines, a mix of Cadillacs and Lincolns, and a half dozen hearses. It was built, Dad told me, as stables for dairy-wagon horses. He grabbed one of the garage's wheeled stretchers and made sure it was equipped. He gathered rubber gloves from a box on a nearby shelving unit, then picked up a plastic brick and said, "This goes under the head." He unzipped the cloth pouch fastened to the top of the stretcher and showed me a plastic sheet lined with boards and outfitted at each corner with heavy-duty nylon handles. "This is the Reeves," he said. "We'll need this if she's on the second floor." And last he grabbed a folded white bedsheet. "This is to cover her if they don't let us take the sheet she's lying on." When these things were set, Dad swung open the back of the hearse and rolled the stretcher up to it. "Look under here," he said and showed me the lever underneath the stretcher that would unlock its legs. He squeezed it. The legs gave way so that half of the weight of the empty stretcher—maybe ten pounds—was in his hands. He rolled the stretcher in and closed the door. "You ready for this?" he said. Part of me was happy just to be spending time with my father outside of our house. Maybe picking up dead bodies together could be our chance to hang out. "Yep," I said. He nodded and got into the hearse and I followed and he drove us away into the night.

Our childhood, my sister's and mine, changed in one day. We were "normal," happyish, and then in one afternoon a kind of violence occurred, and we became the opposite. In one little five-minute window when I was fourteen everything changed. And changed the next twenty years of my life.

My hands shook as we pulled up in front of a tiny row home on another treeless Northeast Philadelphia street. I was cold (no topcoats had been dropped on me), but much more so I was scared. I wasn't so good with corporal realities, was cursed with far too many useless sensitivities. As a boy I had thrown up at the sight of a contortionist on *The Merv Griffin Show*. One lunchtime when I was maybe five I gripped the rim of the kitchen sink and gagged when my mother told me her sandwich was cold meat loaf and ketchup. As a toddler I vomited if I got too close to my sister's diaper changes. On drives to the Poconos I enjoyed getting motion sick and throwing up all over myself. I continue to be afraid of most animals with tails, including cats, rats, mice, monkeys, and especially possums. I hate the zoo. One winter night, when I was fifteen, while putting out the trash in the alley next to our house—I had backed out the door because I was talking to my mother in the kitchen and putting trash in the can was something I could have done blindfolded—I sensed something looking at me, and when I turned, the tips of my fingers, reaching for the can's lid, were maybe an inch from the wide eyes of a possum. A cat would have scrambled away, but this thing stared, perfectly still. In the half second before I skipped frantically back into the house, I believe it made a claim on my soul. I collapsed on my side on the living room floor, kicking myself around in a circle. I came to rest as a tensed ball, the soft insides of my elbow and knee joints clamped tight, and I emitted little moaning cries while my mother stood over me. "Grow up," she said. This is all to say I was one of the least likely young men to wind up among the inherent repugnancies of handling corpses. Even worse, my dad had told me about hazards such as loose bowels and the tissue-thin skin of old people that tore in his hands. And I had never seen this thing called a removal. I didn't know how intricate or demanding it would be. I feared making my debut in front of a family I imagined as agitated and suspicious. I was a wreck.

Dad went into the house first, alone, to carry out some basic reconnaissance. This meant extending his and the funeral director's condolences to the family, but, more important for us,

learning if the body was upstairs or down, whether the weight
of the body was manageable for two men, were there excesses
of blood or shit to deal with, was the body in bed, on the floor,
in the tub, on the toilet. While he did this, I sat in the passenger
seat of the hearse and tried to calm myself with the radio: "Hey,
guys, great topic tonight," a caller said. "My answer is, sure, I
would let Iverson babysit my kids." At twenty-two, I tried to
spend every waking minute accompanied by noise. The sports
talk station I listened to, 610-AM, had adopted its format when
I was in the sixth grade, and from the first week I was a reli-
gious listener. Maybe once a month, Gazz, another friend, Wilbur, or I would call the others and say, "Turn on your radio."
The week before, I had alerted them like this and then made
it on the air with Howard Eskin, the self-proclaimed king of
afternoon drive time in Philadelphia. "Hey, Howard," I'd said
in a cartoonish mimic of the most nasal, vowel-shifted Philly
accent I could manage. "Longtime caller, first-time listener.
My question is this, it's more of a technical question—"

"Okay," he said.

"That yellow line across the field they put on TV to mark
the first downs—"

"Yeah?" he said.

"Do the players ever trip over that?"

He hung up on me and, thanks to the station's seven-second
delay, I turned up the radio to tape my call.

"Great call, genius," Eskin said. "You know what you call
a guy like that?" he asked his audience. "A zero who wants to
be a one. That's what that guy is. A zero trying to be a one."

After a few minutes Dad came outside. I got out of the car, and when he got close, he said, "It's an easy one." I dismissed this as a friendly lie. We rolled the stretcher out of the hearse, and as we neared the front door he asked if I was okay. I nodded yes. My voice would have betrayed me. The truth, though, was that no matter how scared I was, and no matter how little we talked anymore, no matter how much I resented him for how miserable our house was or however much I blamed him for my being a fuckup, I would have followed him anywhere. He was my hero and the man who had killed my mother emotionally. His was the screen onto which all of my love and dread were projected. Is his life now what mine will look like? If I have kids, will I fuck them up? Why does he keep living in our house? What does he think of me? What does he think I should do to get out of this ditch? Why doesn't he just do something to make us normal again? Of course I could never really ask him any of these questions. Much better to keep them to myself and be satisfied with whatever comfort came from physical proximity. In fact this was the model our family existed on. We know we love each other, and we know we aren't equipped to speak of messy feelings, so short of that let's live together in this little house and let nearness stand in as its own form of talking.

My deepest wish, the thing I lived for without being able to articulate it to myself, what I should've outgrown sooner, the dream I held in the deepest corner of my heart's vault, was that one day I'd walk into the house and my parents would be holding hands and tell me, "We've figured it out. We're all

17

right." I wanted this for them on the loftiest planes of spiritual health and romance and lost time redeemed. And, of course, I wanted it for me. I felt broken, that I might have been made permanently too sad by the death of their relationship to ever do anything with my life. The evidence of such was adding up. I couldn't stay in school. I'd never had a real girlfriend. I mostly stayed in my room and I wasn't a teenager anymore. Parents' marriages go bad all the time and people adjust and move on, but there was a stillborn quality to my parents' split. Because they hadn't split. They'd lost that loving feeling in 1990 but stayed together. Instead they kept quiet. They shared a bedroom narrower than the sum of their wingspans. Joyless, they endured. I was certain I would never leave the orbit of their trouble. I had already tried and failed.

Dad was right. My first removal was a breeze. In a hospital bed in the living room, dressed in a nightgown and pink cardigan, lay an eighty-pound sliver of an old woman. Her hands were folded on her chest, with a set of glassy blue rosary beads spilled out between her fingers, pooling on her stomach like jelly beans. Her face had the look of someone fooling a toddler by pretending to sleep. It occurred to me that if Mister Rogers had made an episode about the death of a grandparent, he could have filmed a ride-along with us that night. There's Fred, pervy McFeely, Lady Elaine Fairchilde, all in black suits, squeezed thigh to thigh across the bench seat of the hearse between Dad and me. To make things even more serene, Dad had convinced the woman's family to stay in the kitchen while we worked—I heard murmurs and nose blowing—so only I saw how he leveled the stretcher to the height of her bed, only I witnessed his technique of using her off-white flannel fitted sheet so we could lift her body without ever touching it. It was as if the corpse disposition gods were luring me in with the perfect removal. If it's possible to be spoiled spending a Friday night picking up a dead body for thirty-five dollars, that first one did it. No overpowering odors. No gore. No wailing family. I was like a kid soldier seeing a Bob Hope show on my first day in Vietnam.

When I got home I called Gazz.

"Guess what I did tonight," I said.

"What's that?"

"Had sex."

"Really?" His low, slow voice traveled higher and faster than I'd ever heard it.

"No. I picked up a body with my dad."

"Ah, you did one?" he said, his voice back to normal. I had told him the day before about the black suit.

"Yeah, it was easy."

"And you can keep this job when you go back to school?"

"Yeah, I think so," I said, but I was lying. He rooted for me to finish college. He'd dropped out to work full-time when Kelly got pregnant three years earlier, when we were nineteen. I didn't want to disappoint him, but I wasn't going back to school. I had been bad at it for so long. I was humiliated and confused by my failures. Whatever was wrong with me, I was beginning to understand, was bigger than school. I would walk around campus many days with a lump in my throat. I couldn't concentrate enough to write a paper, and so when a paper was due I wouldn't write it, then not show up to class out of shame. And then I would stop going to the class altogether. But I wouldn't withdraw. I would just let the F happen. I'd flunked out three times from two different schools the past few years. It all felt out of my control, that I used to be a good student and now I wasn't, no matter my best intentions.

———

After I'd done those two removals with my father, I became permanent staff at Livery of Frankford. I was given a beeper and a key to the garage. I was in the general population of removal men, available to go out for a body with one of the fifteen or so regulars, or if the deceased were in a hospital or a nursing home, I'd have to go by myself. And I was available to work funerals, too.

My first was at the church I'd grown up attending, St. Joachim's. I was assigned a job with a title that described every-thing about my present life. As the livery company's secretary, an older woman named Genevieve, had told me on the phone the afternoon before, "You'll be working as an extra man." When I showed up, a group of black suits was gathered in a circle in the church parking lot: hearse driver, limousine driver for the family, flower car driver, and a few who would, like me, be serving as extra men. Several of them were in their sev-enties and even early eighties, and the older they were either the more beautiful or the more deformed their souls seemed. If the funeral business was indeed going to replace college for me, then on this morning all the professors emeriti were accounted for.

Stosh: retired cop, gangly, liver-spotted, scab-nosed from "sun cancer," equipped with a toupee seemingly made of corn silk. He told the story of being shot in a corner store holdup in the early fifties by a pack of niggers, and then watching in court as the judge, a banana-nosed Jew, let the supposed trigger man walk for lack of evidence. Stosh was vile. Stosh blustered like a gaping, blistered asshole. Stosh bought me a coffee at the corner store and asked after my father. I felt pangs of like for Stosh. I didn't know what this meant for me. Maybe it was because he was old and harmless-seeming. Stosh made me feel like Neville Chamberlain.

Charlie Beck: jittery, whispery, shrunken. In his early eighties, with a sly sense of humor—he told a few stories that morning and laughed quietly at others with a look of great tight-lipped pleasure—but mainly he worried, mostly about his wife, Sheila. At one point he borrowed Stosh's newfangled cellular phone and checked in with her. "Yes, I'm in the church parking lot. Yes. Well, I'm on a cordless telephone. Yes, that's right." My guess was that he'd been a drunk as a younger man and that over time they'd both come to depend on her short leash. But he worried about everything, not just her. He patted the pockets of his coat five different times to make sure he hadn't left the keys in the hearse. He worried he'd spill water from the flower arrangements he was charged with carrying from the hearse to the altar, so he fairly sprinted them up the side aisle. He kept checking his watch, worried that mass would run long and we'd hit traffic on the way to the cemetery, even though mass would be ending at eleven in the morning. In one of his few minutes of calm, he told a story about a long-ago removal.

He and his partner lift the woman out of her bed, onto the stretcher, she's light, it's no big deal, he zips up the stretcher pouch, everything's set. They're about to take her out, when in a moment's whisker of stillness, Charlie sees the pouch rise. Ever so faintly. And it falls. Falling faintly and faintly falling. He puts his arm out for his partner to stop. They wait. The pouch rises again. Now he unzips it. The woman's eyes are closed, but he puts his lips to her nostrils and feels the tickle of her breath. He calls the rescue squad. They come. They take her away to the hospital. The next night he picks her up there again. For good. "And you know, the gentleman only paid me once," he says, eliciting from Stosh a cry of "Bullshit!" Charlie says, "Well, sure. Sure. She only died once."

Benny Fogg: another retired cop, carried a miniature .22 on his belt. Just in case. He was cordial to me, and helpful, as were all the men, when I didn't know what I was doing, which was often. Benny blamed the city's unraveling squarely on the niggers, who also, coincidentally, were the problem behind the Eagles' and Phillies' poor play. The Sixers, who hadn't existed before pro sports were integrated, i.e., hadn't been ruined in the men's lifetimes, were mostly ignored in the circle, a lost cause, even though they were the city's most promising team in 1998 and featured Allen Iverson, maybe the most electric player the city had ever seen in any sport. The Flyers had no blacks and were thus capable of stirring only the mildest complimentary conversation. Benny told the story of how a few years back his biceps muscle tore right in half one day while he was pallbearing. He'd never had it fixed, and on this day, for my benefit, he shed his suit coat and flexed the muscle, one lump contracting toward his shoulder and one drooping down to the elbow.

Ronnie: In his well-tailored suit and neatly parted bottle brown hair, he looked like an aging, more suave Pete Rose. He had made a bunch of money selling meat slicers to delis, and since he didn't need the cash he never did removals. He drove limos "just for some action." In a moment when the two of us had a few feet of private space he told me a story, the capsule version of which went: "I drove a kid to his prom last week and his mom gave me a blow job." I didn't solicit further details, mainly because I knew he and my dad were friendly and I didn't want to think of my father alone in a car with any prom kid's mom, but undeterred, Ronnie kept on, the two of us forming our own little circle a few yards from the shadow of the El tracks in the church parking lot where as a boy I'd played gym-class football. He asked me more about myself than any of those guys ever would again. I kept very much to myself, intimidated by the booming talk of the old cops. But Ronnie wasn't put off by my quiet. "You gonna go back to school, And?" "What are you studying?" "You have a girlfriend?" "Why not? Good-looking kid like you."

While the men stood there resolving the world's crises, one or two at a time migrated out to park cars, to put orange paper

"Funeral" stickers on windshields or purple nylon "Funeral" flags with magnetic bases on car roofs, to check out newly arrived hotties in the valuable fifty-four to sixty-nine demographic, to give directions to the cemetery or hand out programs, to carry flower arrangements to the altar or to find the altar boys and give them their three-dollar tips on behalf of the funeral director, and when it was time, to bear the casket out of and later into the hearse, up the steps of the church and later down, and finally, out to the grave. All this executed, in perfect countertension to their downtime patter, with care and respect.

But the one constant was the circle the men formed, and the real conversational entrée, the provider of endless sustenance, was removals. "You wouldn't believe how fat this motherfucker was," Benny said. "We had to get him off the third floor of this hospice out in Lafayette Hill. House must be two hundred years old. No elevator. Just these narrow little winding fucking steps where you have to duck your head. Jesus Christ. I don't know how we did it. We had to slide him down the steps on the Reeves. I'm backing down the steps, the guy's head's right up against my balls. We have a sheet over him but I'm drippin sweat. I drip so much his face starts to show through the sheet. It's like the fucking Shroud of Turin. Jesus Christ."

And then old Stosh picked it up: "We get back to the funeral home—do you know what she gives us? I told her how goddamned hard it was. I told her we could've used at least two extra men out there but we managed anyway. Do you know what she tipped us? Three dollars. An altar boy tip. Three dollars in bills. To split. How do you split three paper dollars? A dumb woman she is. And I like the woman. But she's dumb."

The circle noted which funeral directors wouldn't dole out for breakfast sandwiches during a funeral, which ones called you too late at night for removals and asked you to drive too far without ever giving you more cash, which ones still hadn't put in a ramp after fifty years in business so that on every fucking removal you have to bang the stretcher down the steps and hold the screen door open with your goddamned ass.

My father wasn't there that day, but several of the men, in brief instances when it was just two of us, made sure to ask how he was. They seemed really to like him, and, in the context of the circle, I could see him more clearly. Gentle and not a blowhard like many of them could be. He had read more, but he also was alive to the world in ways many of them weren't. He was a finely tuned sensualist in a lot full of puttering Buicks. If he were there he would have noticed birdsong, cloud shapes suggestive of the profiles of old character actors, changes in light, movie ads on passing buses, the arrivals of subtly sexy women. I knew because I noticed those things that day, and he was sharper than I was. He noticed when a rare bird landed in our yard, but he also knew its name. He kept an Audubon guide by the back door and had taught himself. He knew the names of constellations and when and where to expect them. He knew big chunks of Shakespeare and Whitman and Yeats by heart. *But one man loved the pilgrim soul in you.* This, though, is how my thinking about my father went in these days: appreciation followed without reprieve by resentment, or vice versa. Never anything without strings. And so the next thought was: And all that for what? Into your sixth decade, slinging corpses to pay bills, still in Frankford, still with the low, murmuring gripes from other men about niggers and spics and the cheap Jew owner of the football team flooding like sewage into your little one-man library, an abettor to our degradation, just like twenty years ago, with no money in the bank, with a wife who won't look at you? This is what scared me. Why would I pursue a lowly English degree when it seemed books had changed nothing for my father? Not for the better. We were all drowning.

2

When my sister and I were small, before the house changed, my mother would sit on the edges of our beds and wake us with "sweeswees," her name for light strokes along the undersides of our forearms. I hated to wake up, so I would pull the covers over my head, eject one arm, and cry to her, "I need sweeswees." Sometimes she would rouse me by singing her own words to the verse melody of the *The Jetsons'* theme song: "Come on, Andrew. Time for schoo-ool. Get out of beh-hed. Don't be-e a fool." Downstairs she poured us Cheerios while we listened to a radio show called *Harvey in the Morning*. Harvey, who a few years later would become the announcer on a kids' game show called *Double Dare*, played pop acts like Fleetwood Mac, Stevie Wonder, Paul Simon, Kim Carnes, Todd Rundgren, the Doobies, America, Men at Work. Maybe once an hour he played a stand-up bit by someone like Steve Martin or Richard Pryor, or a skit by Kip Addotta. Mom would pack our lunches and then hand us off to an older girl on the block, Colleen McQueen, who walked us the mile to school. While we were there Mom babysat as a full-time job, watching a few kids whose parents would drop them off at our house on their way to work.

At night, she would often go down to her sewing machine at the front of the cellar, just outside my father's office, and sew curtains and seat covers and pillowcases for the house, and she made dresses for Theresa and shorts and sweatpants for both of us. When long, baggy Hawaiian-print shorts called Jams were popular, in the mid-eighties, Mom made us knock-offs with her leftover fabric, lime-green cotton patterned with smiling purple suns that she had already used to make cushions for the backyard chairs—"It's psychedelic," she told us. When Theresa and I sat on the cushions while wearing our shorts we appeared to float. I was wearing these seat-cushion shorts on the deck of my uncle's house in the Poconos one day when I was so startled and delighted by my older cousin Bernie rip-cording a whole can of Genesee Cream Ale that I soaked the shorts and the deck with a full bladder of pee.

Mom took a night class at a local high school and learned cal-ligraphy. She took another class and learned to make stained-glass panels. She constructed a little workshop for herself at the back of the cellar, under the kitchen, where she would cut shapes from sheets of colored glass and fit the pieces together. The tip of her iron melted the solder, the lead strips bubbling, smelling smoky and spicy like a hundred freshly sharpened pencils. She baked bread and cakes and cookies. She cooked dinner every night. Many nights before we sat down to eat she'd send one of us to deliver a plate, hot and wrapped in foil, to one of the older neighbors on the block. She kept a garden that ran lengthwise in two long beds bordering either side of our small grass backyard. She seemed forever to be painting or wallpapering a different room. She was our Sisyphus of wallpaper, running on nervous energy. She read novels at night. She did needlepoint.

Dad could make her laugh on command. She would ask him to do her favorite impression, of a boy from Dad's high school Spanish class, and he would shoot his arm over his head, bend his hand down at the wrist, wriggle his fingers, and in the same kind of nasally and stretched-out Philadelphia accent I called WIP with, would say, "Haaace frioooo, Padreee." For her benefit he would also recite the lines of a gravely serious priest from an Italian movie they'd watched in Catholic high school in the sixties. "Marcelino Panevino," he would say, imitating the gravely serious American voice-over artist. "Marcelino bread and wine." After dinner and dishes, if Theresa and I had finished our homework, the routine was for all of us to gather in the living room in front of the TV. We'd watch *Entertainment Tonight* at 7:00 and at 7:30 a local show called *Evening Magazine*. On Saturday nights we'd watch *Fame* and *Solid Gold* and *The Muppet Show*. Theresa was a fearless little gymnast, and she'd spin cartwheels, round-offs, and handsprings in the confines of our tiny living room. When *Solid Gold* came on she'd disappear behind the love seat and return with her pants discarded and her underwear pulled up between her butt cheeks to mimic the Solid Gold Dancers' thongs.

We are young and alive and together in these days. We are all in exactly the right place. Theresa and I win prizes for our grades. We are as robust as Granny's rosebush. Theresa is a champion gymnast. I am an all-star first baseman. Flourishing among neighbors and grandparents and aunts and uncles and cousins, we are as vibrantly alive and creeping as the honeysuckle between our yard and Betty Lou's. I have eaten the Eucharist. Mom is slender and beautiful with chestnut hair to her shoulders. She has navigated us both into school and now she's been hired to teach the eighth grade at St. Joachim's. Dad writes poems, plays guitar, sings in the living room, coaches my baseball team, plays softball with the other coaches. We take vacations with family and friends. We are young and alive and we have each other.

———

One day when I was a little boy, my mother tuned the dial to hear Dad read his poems on a local public radio show. It was this day when I first realized that he was two people, specifically, that the act of reading aloud somehow made him a stranger, summoned in him a dark electricity that had no outlet at home. The same transformation happened, I started to see, when, on the rare occasion he joined us at church, he would sing. Especially in the chaste relief of a church pew, there was something in his singing voice, a glimpse offered into some unknown richness, that made my cheeks flush. It was like peering down an open manhole on a quiet street and seeing the North Atlantic. Here was a mystery more piercing than any we're fed in church. Here is a man, a man close to life. He knows things. He loves me. I am of him. Why would I not want to be like him?

The Nicene Creed says, "We believe in one God, the Father, the Almighty, maker of heaven and earth, and of all that is, seen and unseen." Most Sundays my mother would pull my sister and me to church while Dad stayed home and read the sports page under a cloud of bacon smoke. I believed in my father.

———

My first solo pickup I was asleep at 1:00 a.m. when the beeper went off. I woke up and called the answering service and was asked to go to the morgue at Frankford Hospital and pick up a man named Orville. I washed my face with cold water and put on my suit. I was ready for this.

I backed the hearse up to the loading dock. A security guard met me and led the way to the morgue as I pushed the stretcher behind him. When we got there I signed for Orville's death certificate and slid it between the Reeves and the stretcher so it would stay flat and dry. Orville was wrapped in a white plastic pouch, which the guard unzipped in front of me so that we could both read the ID tag, looped around the dead man's toe like a Christmas tree ornament. Orville was long and withered away to the kind of weight—maybe 140—that made handling him easy. And since hospital bodies are cleaned up and kept cold, the remover's senses get a break. Once we were back in the hearse, it was only a mile and a half trip up Frankford Avenue to Wepner's, the funeral home Orville's family had chosen and who in turn had called Livery of Frankford looking for a remover.

Alone in the middle of the night I drove down dark block after block, with a bedroom light on every now and then. I passed an empty bus going the other way. It seemed like I wasn't just the one person awake in the city but the only one alive. I could already sense that inside each removal I would be traversing microclimates of mood, that some minutes of a lonesome, dark trip were exhilarating, almost giddy-making for their desolation and for the sheer craziness of what I found myself doing, and that others needed serious leavening. One way to lighten the night, of course, was the radio.

Before a hearse is chopped to fit its fate, it starts life as a simple luxury car, Cadillac or Lincoln, equipped with power seats, leather everything, icy AC, and, in 1998, a top-of-the-line AM/FM cassette-playing stereo. This particular moment driving Orville up Frankford Ave—the ease of his transport, my interrupted sleep, my lifelong familiarity with this strip of road skewed by the radical novelty of my traveling companion—left me feeling fuzzed out, high on the buzz of my singular circumstance. I was feeling deeply Orville, deeply 2:00 a.m., deeply superior to anyone waking up for college or a regular job in a few hours. I was feeling deeply Pavement.

"Type Slowly" comes on. "Sing it, Orville!" I yell, before I croon along with Malkmus, *"'One of us is a cigar stand / and one of us is / a lovely blue incandescent guillotine.'* You nailed it, Orville!" We're at a red light at Frankford and Devereaux. Do you know what happened at Frankford and Devereaux seventy-two years ago, Orville? I bet you do. Maybe you were there. The Frankford Yellow Jackets won the NFL Championship. Their stadium was right here where there's a Burger King and a used car lot and a park that women don't walk through alone. Imagine Frankford with its own NFL team. Not Philadelphia's team, but Frankford's. Nineteen twenty-six. Four years after the elevated train reached Frankford, so people from all over the city could come to games. More than half a decade before the Eagles were even a zygote swimming in the city's mind. One of the Yellow Jackets' stars that season, Orville, was a halfback whose money plays were touchdown passes, a twenty-five-year-old named Houston Stockton, from a Jesuit college all the way out in Washington State called Gonzaga. He would one day be the grandfather of another Gonzaga product, a man who would become famous in the 1990s for the 1926-style part in his hair, for the way he threw his elbows at opponents' noses and crotches like a football player, for his grandfathered ball-hugger shorts, and, unlike his grandfather, for his failure to win a championship, a man named John Stockton, who played for the Utah Jazz and would make the Basketball Hall of Fame on the strength of his passing. What's that you say about apples falling near the trees, Orville?

The song ends. I hear something. I eject the tape. I squint to hear better. The sound comes again, but this time it's louder. A long, guttural "Aaaaaaah." Orville is moaning. I'm being punished for making him sing. I was kidding, Orville. I consider the possibility: Did the pronouncing doctor get this wrong? Is there a dead man alive in the car with me? "Orville, please stop," I say. "Please stop, Orville." I am alone, I tell myself. This person is *dead*. The light turns green, and when the hearse moves again his moaning grows louder and stronger. And then stops. We're almost to the funeral home. Orville is almost returned to the state of existence in which he spent every one of his living days: not my problem. He lets out another moan so low, so long I feel tears coming. "Orville, please!" It's 2:00 a.m. on a weeknight. My fingers are shaking on the steering wheel of a silver hearse. I am pleading with a dead man to leave me in peace.

I back up to the garage at Wepner's. I open the back door of the hearse. Slowly. My body is a single section of quivering bowel. Orville appears still. I'm sweating. Before I can put my hands on the stretcher to pull him out of the car, I take four deep breaths. What if he moves? What if he talks to me? I need this to be done before he talks again. I am expert at avoiding talks. I turn and punch in the garage door code I've been given by the answering service. When the door has finally receded up into the ceiling of the garage, I take a last breath and then yank the stretcher and race us inside. In the funeral home's morgue I pull Orville's body bag from the stretcher onto the embalming table. I let myself breathe. I could leave at this point. Part of me is screaming, "Leave!" I've brought the body in. I've earned my thirty-five bucks. But I need to see him. I could argue it's for his sake. If he's alive he needs to go back to the hospital. But I don't do it for him. I'm discovering that something in me craves the most baleful havoc this job can produce. If I'm a dinghy moored to my sad parents, to Frankford, to my own mounting failures, then maybe this job can snap the rope, blow me clear of real life's dock, push me far, far away into some fantasy ether and leave all this drudgery shrinking at the horizon. I want this dead man to spring up and try to kill me, or at least wake up singing "Hello, It's Me." Something. Anything. I peel the bag back slow. Before I unveil his face, the part of me that wants to run takes one last dose of courage from the thought that if Orville's eyes are open and focused on me then I will die instantly from a heart attack and not have to worry about him anymore.

I start to believe Orville's dead when I see his eyelids three-quarters closed and perfectly still—a trick the living can't pull off—exposing only milky undercrescents of eyeball. He doesn't sit up or yawn. I put my gloved fingers on his bare chest. It's still. I don't have the guts like Charlie to put my lips to him to feel for breath. Instead I pinch his forearm. Nothing. I am fairly certain he is among the deceased. When I've washed my hands I look at him one more time. "Orville," I say, "I'm leaving now." His eyes stay closed.

I drive back to the garage in silence. At some point along Frankford Ave I realize I don't want the night to end. Removals, these visits I now find myself making to the membrane between life and death, don't feel anything like I'd expected. The dead are becoming the most vivid people in my life. They are for sure the only ones whose chests I'm touching.

———

French I, freshman year of high school. There's a bookcase in the back of the room filled with recent copies of *Paris Match*. Father Kibbie runs the class in a loose way, meaning he leaves large chunks of "study time" during which we're beseeched to do French homework or read the magazines. I can remember many days sitting at my desk egging on a full erection incited by nude beach candids of Brigitte Nielsen. During one of these study sessions, something wet hits the back of my neck. A little wad of balled-up loose leaf, gummy from spit. I turn around and see a kid with spiky, flaxen hair who looks like Alvin if he'd borrowed Simon's glasses, a kid Father Kibbie calls Mr. Gazz because he can't pronounce Gansawnkaja. Gazz just smiles at me, still holding his hollowed-out Bic pen, not even trying to feign innocence.

———

The morning after Orville, I went into the kitchen while Dad, in a T-shirt, sweatpants, and moccasins, stood over a frying pan.

"You want scrapple, buddy?" he said.

Wondrous earthy perfume, frying scrapple. To eat it—a pressed loaf of cornmeal and the slaughterhouse oddments of pig: tail, skin, stomach, snout—is to want not.

"A guy moaned at me last night," I said. I pulled the ketchup from the fridge and put it on the table. I sat down.

"What do you mean?"

"The body I picked up. It was talking. Like, 'Aaaaaaaaah.'"

"Ooh, boy." He set in front of me a plate of scrambled eggs bordered by four piping brown slices of the stuff, each a third of an inch thick and as wide and long as a playing card.

"Yeah, I've had that happen to me once," he said.

"Really?"

He sat down and doused the contents of his plate with the ketchup. He slid the bottle to me, and I did the same. Forking into a properly prepared slice of scrapple is like cracking into crème brûlée: a thin, brittle, slightly scorched shell gives way to custard.

"You think he was totally dead, right?" I said. Never more than when I ate scrapple in these early days of removals did it occur to me that I was becoming the creature I feared most: the possum. I left the house at night, skulking around in shadow to clear away a dead thing. Now here I was eating the swept-up scraps off the abattoir floor, the breakfast equivalent of roadkill, feeling more myself with every bite.

"Yeah, it's just gas leaving the body," he said. "Passes over the vocal cords." These had become the kinds of things we talked about, now that we were coworkers, over breakfast.

An October Monday, 1990. I was fourteen, a sophomore at Northeast Catholic High School. My sister was in the seventh grade at St. Joachim's. We got home around the same time that day and noticed that Dad was already home. This was strange, him home before five. I thought he must've had a class canceled. We didn't see him, but his school bag was where he always put it when he got in, on the dining room chair at the end of the buffet, and we saw the cellar light on, so assumed he was down there working in his office. "Dad?" I called down the stairs. "I'll be up," he said.

I poured the first of several bowls of Acme-brand Cheerios and took my spot at the kitchen table, my head in the *Inquirer* sports page as usual, reading the bits I hadn't gotten to before school, items like golf, boxing, high school soccer capsules. Eventually Mom came home from work. "Dad's home," I said to her and kept reading. She went down the cellar steps, and neither of them surfaced for a long time. Mom came up first. I was reading and the cellar door was behind my seat, so I didn't see her before she disappeared upstairs to their bedroom. Dad came up a few minutes later, and I turned to look at him when he did. His eyes were red. He wiped his nose with his handkerchief. He was out of his work clothes—usually a suit—and had changed into a green sweatshirt and jeans. Weird to see him dressed casually on a weekday afternoon. He said, "Hi, buddy," to me in a whisper. He didn't linger. He went right upstairs, too, and I could hear him close the bedroom door.

The closing of the door resonated in me as powerfully as, was as rare as, somehow more unusual than, my father emerging from the cellar on a Monday afternoon crying. My parents' bedroom door was never closed. They changed with it open, my mother using the angle of wall and in-let door like a dressing screen. They slept with it open. They wanted to hear what was going on in the house. They eschewed a window air conditioner even on the hottest summer night; the room's closed windows and door and the noise from the machine would prevent them hearing the street and the house. They were always monitoring. Always looking out for us.

Theresa came into the kitchen and said, "What do you think's wrong with Dad?"

"Someone died," I said. "Or Dad has cancer."

She nodded. I hadn't formulated some great insight. Our neighbor, Mrs. Hollins, was our parents' age, and the mother of a girl, Katie, and boy, Richie, whose ages matched my sister's and mine. Katie was my sister's best friend. Richie and I were different—I played sports as a little kid, he played G.I. Joe— but we were close, like family. We didn't have to hang out every day; we had shared bathwater. Mrs. Hollins had what looked like a summer buzz cut, and in the last weeks before she died of cancer her cheeks sunk in. That was 1986. My mother's mother had been sick in the late seventies with colon cancer and had spent June 1990 in the hospital having her bladder removed. Cancer wasn't new to us. It was something that happened.

Our parents stayed in their bedroom for a long time. Mom came down a while after our regular dinnertime and asked me to heat up leftovers for Theresa and me. She went back to their room. We didn't see Dad again that night. He was in bed Tuesday when we went to school. When we got home, he was in the cellar again. He ate dinner with us Tuesday. His eyes were still red. Wednesday was the same. Neither Theresa nor I asked any questions. I was afraid of what the answers would be. He was in bed again when we left for school Thursday. When we got home, he was sitting at the kitchen table. He looked sick. He was pale. I think I would rather have gone on having whatever was wrong be kept secret than have to sit at the kitchen table and talk to our suffering father. No member or element of the family's dynamic was equipped for communicating emotion. Dad put his in poems we rarely saw. Mom put hers into moods that rose and fell like the barometer. She was our atmosphere. She regulated pressure. A thunderstorm was a surly housecleaning with our unhung coats hurled down the cellar steps. A sunny day was brownies. Theresa and I weren't yet required to process emotions of much weight. For physical pain, we were both still young enough for tears to be okay. We had gone through the death of both of Dad's parents, of Mrs. Hollins, and of our next-door neighbor Miss Hippel. We had cried. But we were young enough to run around and play with cousins and friends at the funeral luncheons. Neither of us had ever felt anything that lingered, never felt anything strong enough to survive an ice cream cone or a night's sleep.

Mrs. Browning was sitting up in bed, like she'd been reading. She wore a wig that re-created the sandy brown bob I'd known her to favor. Her face was drawn. She weighed less than a hundred pounds, which was maybe forty lighter than she had in the eighties, but she was perfectly recognizable. Every week of first, second, and third grade, our class would visit Mrs. Browning for an hour in the school library. We'd sit at her feet on a sand-colored utility carpet, and she'd read to us from books like *Mike Mulligan and His Steam Shovel* and *Babar Saves the Day*. When she finished we were allowed to spend the remaining time reading anything we liked. I would always pull out old sports encyclopedias, their spines held together by electrical tape. Over and over I read the entries for people like Jim Thorpe, Bronko Nagurski, Gertrude Ederle. I remember a black-and-white photo of Ederle standing on a beach, smeared in Vaseline, ready to cross the English Channel. One of my favorite entries belonged to the Galloping Ghost, Red Grange. When he was playing college ball at Illinois, before he was the Ghost, he was called the Wheaton Ice Man for his summer job hauling blocks of ice. I gravitated to athletes with day jobs. I grew up knowing that Johnny Callison, a star Phillies right fielder of the 1960s, had spent his winters tending bar in Philadelphia. In high school I read everything I could about Wallace Stevens after I found out he'd worked as an insurance executive. People like him made me think of my dad, who worked as a teacher but whose true calling was poetry.

Driving Mrs. Browning back to the funeral home, I started to think, What if I stay in this job long enough that eventually I pick up all my old teachers, all our old neighbors, all the priests whose masses I'd served, all my baseball and soccer coaches, my mother's parents, my aunts and uncles, and then, of course, my mother and my father? What if I collect the adults of my childhood like I'm curating a museum of my own history? What if I have them stuffed and cast in representative settings? Look, there's my grandmother scratching a lottery ticket. There are my uncles with their heads thrown back at the punch line of a Jew joke. There's my mother on a kneeler begging for our souls. There's my father in the backyard with his shirt off reading Whitman. There's my father standing in the living room—he's thirty-five, with black hair and a black mustache—on a summer afternoon watching the Phillies play on TV while he teaches himself the banjo. There's my father carrying a corpse down a flight of stairs. There's my father—he's older now, forty-five, graying, paunchy—in front of the television making a lupine call at the sight of a starlet on *Entertainment Tonight*.

And then that day comes for my sister and me, the day that fixes our befores and afters. A Thursday afternoon, three days after Dad has emerged from the basement red-eyed. Now he sits at the kitchen table. He's been waiting for us to get home.

I have spent two months of the previous spring and summer immobilized by a leg broken playing softball in my school shoes with other members of the concert band. (My fourteen-year-old clarinetist self would want you to know that I stayed in the game after the injury, thinking it was just a bruise, lined a double to left, and scored a run before my knee blew up.)

Since I wasn't walking, I had spent most of the summer before sophomore year inside watching television and reading newspapers. And eating like a just-released POW. I wasn't seeing friends, except the few that came by to sign my cast. I wasn't meeting girls. I didn't have chronically bad skin, but I was prone to that one red, shiny, almost-glowing pimple on the tip of my growing nose. In that one summer my hair had gone from chestnut and wavy, the kind that aunts and grandmothers coo over and stroke, to a coarse, tightly curled, whopping bush of pubic-grade steel wool that in my fourteen-year-old wisdom I wore grown out long enough to hang in front of one eye. I was sullen. Aggressively, infectiously sullen. Despite a placid home, where I had never seen my parents fight. Despite Mass every Sunday.

Dad was in his normal dinner seat at the drop-leaf maple table. Theresa's usual spot was lost during the day—her leaf was dropped, the table pushed against the wall, out of the way of kitchen traffic—so she sat at Mom's place. I sat in my usual chair, across the table from Dad. I don't think any of the three of us breathed much. I can't remember being that uneasy again in my life. Finally he started.

"Something happened at school," he said.

It wasn't cancer. I jumped to: "laid off." I had heard of lots of friends' dads being laid off. I ran through the names of all the local colleges I knew from the sports pages. There must be a hundred colleges around Philadelphia. He could find work quick.

"A few women students . . . ," he said.

Such a lovely sunny day. Mom had wallpapered the room yellow and made curtains, yellow with white vertical stripes. She'd covered the seat cushions for the kitchen chairs with the same material. The kitchen's two windows looked onto the narrow alley we shared with Betty Lou, our next-door neighbor, so even at midday the room was never filled with sunlight. But that day the room radiated.

"Said that I touched their knees or put my hands on their shoulders." He blew his nose. He always carried one of his handkerchiefs in his back pocket. I took pride in folding them the way he liked: in half; in half sideways; in thirds sideways; clap it tight.

"La Salle is firing me for sexual harassment."

Stained-glass pieces Mom had made hung in most rooms of the house: a dolphin suncatcher in my bedroom window; a transom light over the porch door that read "Meredith"; and, at my father's back as we sat at the table, in the door between the kitchen and the back shed, a panel depicting two tulips in bloom.

He took a deep breath. "I want you both to know I love you very much."

My eyebrows lifted as high as shock could take them. Theresa stood up. Dad stood up. They went into a strong, sniffling embrace. I knew my place was to latch myself on to their hug. I couldn't stand up. I thought instead. I didn't feel capable of any unconditional feelings. Already I was replaying the words: "touched their knees." Even at fourteen I sensed a false note. If I'd lost my job of sixteen years over something as stupid as touching someone's knee, I'd be throwing lamps against the wall. Maybe I'd cry like he was, but more than anything there'd be rage at the unfairness, and I wouldn't need three days of hiding before I told my kids. And those words—"I love you"—had never been said to me before that moment. I had never heard my mother say it. I had heard my father say it once or twice to my sister when she was a toddler, but only when she had said it first, she calling it down the hallway after he'd tucked her in. They didn't feel important, those words, at least not as an indicator of how much our parents loved us, which always felt too big for words. It felt as if Dad was using them now to mean, "Please help me." I'm sure he needed on a molecular level to have those words in the air in the house. I told myself to stand up. I stood up. I could sense that Dad was waiting for me to join the hug. Theresa's head was lost against his chest. He watched me. I was fourteen; I didn't like hugs on a normal day. I made my way glacially around the small table. The door to the dishwasher was open. Dad must have been unloading it when we came in. I stepped around the door. I stood behind my sister and opened my arms wide enough to clear her body and touch Dad's. My eyes were the only part of me that wanted to be open; every other muscle felt tight and stiff and closing down. I thought. Mom knows, right? Of course she knows. How will she be? What will her family say? The people we know who go to La Salle—my cousin, our neighbor, my friend's sister—what will they say? Everybody we know will know because of them. Because I knew how the last three days had been: secrecy, silence, evasion, sugarcoating; because I had never seen my parents fight or discuss anything of consequence; because they had never given me a talk—no primers on sex, dating, kissing, drugs, booze; there was an instinct in me that knew, even as we were hugging, that this was it, that the family as it had been was over. No getting past this trauma. None of us were equipped. The hug broke up. Dad stayed in the kitchen. He'd finish unloading the dishwasher. Theresa would go upstairs to her room. I would go to mine. I would lie on my bed waiting for the sound of Mom coming home.

I'm four years old. A spring morning, 1980. I'm in the passenger seat. Dad's driving me to my babysitter, Betty. The radio says, "I saw the light in your eyes." When he's ready for another Camel, Dad lets me push in the lighter. I'm learning street names. We live on Oakland. Betty lives on Oxford. Everything I see has always been here. The sycamore tree out front, the brick Sears tower on Roosevelt Boulevard, the signs that hang like backwards *L*s over the front doors of corner buildings that say "Pat's"; "Dell's"; "Heron's"; one that just says "Tavern."

The row of cars at the curb is breaking up. People leaving the rows of houses, going away to work. One pulls out in front of us too close. Dad punches the brake. He throws the soft side of his forearm in front of my chest to hold me against the seat. "Asshole," he says. "It's okay, buddy," he says to me.

We're at a red light on Oxford Avenue by a graveyard. Lots of graveyards on this drive. A lady walks across the street in front of us. She has short hair. She's wearing tight jeans and high heels. She's younger than Mom. Dad's tongue makes a noise like a motorcycle rev. I try to make my mouth a motorcycle but it comes out "brum."

Looking back: He teaches creative writing at La Salle College, the school he graduated from in 1970. He's getting poems published in literary journals of increasing prestige. He's thirty-two years old. He's been married to my mother for eight years but known her eighteen, since a picnic on Labor Day, 1962—the day before they started high school. He was fourteen. She was thirteen. It's hard to shake the feeling of predestination around here. Predictability, though, will not do in a poem. She's the little sister of the girl his big brother almost married. He's the fourth of five. She is, too. Big Catholic families get all wrapped up and tangled around here, and even the brightest kids wind up not ever getting too far away. A few years ago he was studying poetry at the University of Florida with John Ciardi and James Dickey, and now he's back in Frankford, driving on the Boulevard to La Salle past St. Martin's, where he was baptized, where the Mass of Christian Burial will have been performed for both his parents before six more years pass. The Church is part of his tangle even more than he knows. And he knows it plenty.

Marian. The girl he married. My mother. She goes into the convent out of high school. He writes her letters. She leaves the nuns after six years. He marries her. The day after the wedding they leave for Gainesville. He would've been happy to take the best job he could find after he graduated. Let his pedigree take him somewhere new in America. He's never seen much of the country. Marian wants to have babies and raise them near her parents and sisters. He gets an offer at La Salle. It's 1974. They find an apartment in Northeast Philadelphia. I'm born in 1975. A few days before Christmas 1976 they buy a row house in Frankford. The house is one mile from her parents and one mile from his. It's one block from her father's childhood home, one block from her mother's. I'm baptized in St. Joachim's, the same church where my mother, her brothers and sisters, and her parents were baptized. In the spring of 1980 her mother is knocked down for her purse while she's shopping on Frankford Avenue, by Frankford Hospital, under the Frankford El. By Christmas 1980 her parents have moved across the Delaware to a single home in New Jersey. Her sisters are moving away, too. It's starting to feel to him like they came back here for nothing. But now he has two kids. He's been at La Salle six years. Raises and promotions are coming. But everything seems smaller all the time. He loves and hates the Christian Brothers who run La Salle for the same reasons he loves and hates his wife. They need other people. They believe. They cling to what they know.

He is thirty-two. He is thin and finally handsome. A late-blooming man with talent he's just beginning to control. A talent no one else in the neighborhood cares about. He watches the woman cross in front of his car. His tongue rolls. He can't help himself. He's reminding himself what he's given up. He wants the boy to know, too. He purrs at the shape of her. He's a lion. The light goes green.

———————

There is so much I don't remember. Not Mom coming home that day, or dinner that night, if I slept well, anything about school the following morning. My next memory is of being at work the next day, after school, in the rectory of the priests who taught us. Every Friday afternoon I would go to their house adjacent to the school and clean the bathrooms. It was a tan brick building, three stories, just like Carl's, as long as a short city block, connected to the high school by an open-air bridge between the second floors. It was built in 1933 along with the school, Northeast Catholic High School for Boys, in a time when the sons of European immigrants flooded Catholic schools, and so there were bedrooms for scores of priests and several large communal bathrooms.

By 1990 the student body and the number of priests had dwindled. The rectory was less than half full. The hall lights were kept off in daytime, and, on cloudy days especially, desolation prevailed. It rained the day after Dad told us of his firing. I was still wearing my eyebrows high on my forehead. I must've looked like that all day in class, too. Along with shock there was another new feeling, something different from the hormonal crankiness I'd been soaking in for the past six months. I had become aware of every step I took, every swipe of the mop, every reach for a rag or bottle. I remember looking out the rectory's bathroom windows at passing El trains and thinking, There's an El car. There's another El car. There's another El car. Anything like ease had gone from my brain and I felt as if I had moved into some inner chamber of myself where I observed everything but couldn't be seen. Inside that command center the video monitors ran a steady loop of thoughts: the replay of Dad telling us, me wishing the four of us could go back to the time before he did, knowing the wish would always fail.

My French teacher, Father Kibbie, was also in charge of the rectory, where he maintained an office as wide as two bedrooms, in the middle of the second floor. He was rarely in when I pushed my bucket by, but his door was always left open, shades drawn. Next to his desk in the permanent dusk of that old room a parrot perched in a cage. I would stop and look at him from the hallway, and he would regard me, too. A few times, when I was down the hall, out of sight, I'd heard him talk to Father Kibbie, but in all the times I'd stopped to eye him he'd never said a word.

I knew that parrots could live close to a hundred years, and I wondered what if this weren't Father Kibbie's animal but had been in the room since 1933, passed down as a gift for each new head of the community. How many men had sat at that desk in sixty years and talked to him, spilled themselves in ways they wouldn't to their fellow priests, the way one could only to a lover or a best friend? How many whispered names of longed-for men and women had he heard, how many doubts? How many joys, shared with this dull green bird, had taken on a sadness merely in the circumstance of their telling?

———

Only a few months went by while Dad was out of work. One semester he was teaching at La Salle, the next semester he was teaching at a community college in New Jersey. He might have been making half as much money and had lost his health insurance, but his exposure to public humiliation was mostly over. He was working, and no one seemed even to notice that he'd switched jobs. If they did, maybe they thought he'd been a victim of layoffs.

———

Circumstantial evidence:

Because of how invested she was in her religion, with its intolerance of divorce; because a teacher at a Catholic grade school, with no union on her side, could be fired at the whim of the pastor for getting divorced; because of how little money she made; because of the shame of disappointing her happily married parents; because of her faith in my father finding his way; because of her wanting my sister and me to grow up with both parents, my mother stuck it out. She stayed.

It never felt natural for one day.

The word *crisis* comes from the Greek, meaning "choice," but my sister and I grew up thinking it meant the opposite. It meant a fate imposed and not to be questioned. It meant something bad happens and you endure it. It meant a permanent repeating of private humiliation. It meant no choice at all.

It occurred to me at some point not long after he was fired and they stopped talking to each other—maybe it was when I was reading *Death of a Salesman* for class—that because I became so aware of when my father or mother entered a room, home often felt like we were onstage. *Enter Dad stage right. Mom sighs, exits stage left.* In effect, we had lost our house as a home. The place we lived was now the least comfortable, the least private place any of us occupied in a day. We went to school and work to relax and be alone and be ourselves. At least my sister and I had our own bedrooms. Our parents had no respite.

If this was true, that the communal spaces in the house were all a stage, then my cassettes were switchblades that let me slice through the backdrop and step into a darkness where no one could see me. Or maybe this: If the depression that had started to grow in me felt like being locked in a command center full of surveillance monitors, then music opened a door from that room into a second room, a tiny, womb-like space with a bed and low ceilings painted gray. In this room I could forget myself, sleep if I wanted, let my body grow. And when I would forget myself, I would realize that the bands I loved—R.E.M. and the Smiths, mostly—were, elementally, families making sounds together. They were my families, these people I'd never met.

Only a few weeks after the firing, Father Kibbie fell from a ladder and shattered his heel.

This meant that French II moved to a classroom that could

accommodate his wheelchair. In the new room's arrangement I found myself seated next to Mr. Gazz. I didn't know much about him—he was on the soccer team and the back of my head was his spitball target—and I didn't like him. But we got used to each other. One day he was filling out a form to get free cassettes from Columbia House. He was ordering tapes by the Smiths, Joy Division, Siouxsie and the Banshees, all groups that I thought I was the only kid in the room who liked. It seemed like every other boy at North, nearly 100 percent of them white, only liked hip-hop. I liked it too, but my freshman year there had been a melee between white kids and a few of the school's only black kids, and by this year, nearly all the black kids had left. I found it maddening that in a place that felt so unwelcoming to blacks, everybody wanted to be a rapper. My sympathies and my underdeveloped sense of irony drove me to the whitest music around. Pretty soon Gazz and I had turned our corner of French class into a private booth. It wasn't just the same music we loved. We spent time that should have been devoted to the passé composé passing jokes about local sportscasters, sharing story notes on the previous night's episode of *Thirtysomething*, wondering how we'd make it until the new R.E.M. album came out. Once his soccer season ended, we got into the habit of talking every day after school, too, while he waited at the bus stop. One day it came up—he told me not in any way meant to win sympathy, just as an answer to a question about his family—that when he was twelve his nine-year-old brother had died from leukemia. Right away I loved him more than before. Right away the ritual that marked our daily parting—his bus approaching, us nodding a farewell, the both of us reaching for our headphones before turning away—made more sense.

———————

Theresa's bedroom had a window air conditioner, so on the hottest summer nights I slept on her floor. One night in June 1991—she was twelve, I was fifteen—she woke me up. "Look at my eye," she said. It was swollen shut like a boxer's. She'd already been awake examining it in the bathroom. Now it was the two of us. She sat on the toilet lid in her boxer shorts and tank top crying soft enough not to wake Mom and Dad. She threw up in the toilet and then sat back down on it. The flesh around her eye grew while she sat there until it was bulbous like a fly's eye. I remember this sense of dread in my stomach, not just that she was sick but that our parents couldn't take another calamity.

The next morning Mom took her to the pediatrician, and from there to the emergency room. At first doctors thought she'd been bitten by a spider. Several days later someone concluded she had a staph infection in the orbital bone around her left eye. In the middle of her hospital stay I went to Nags Head as the one Meredith representative on what had been planned as our family vacation with the Hallers, my parents' best friends, and their kids. I spent the week as only a selfish child could, lost in Wiffle ball and basketball games and on crabbing expeditions where we would tie a length of twine around a rotten chicken leg and drag it slowly through the low tide waters of Oregon Inlet. When we got back to Philadelphia, Theresa was out of the hospital and healing from surgery to reduce the swelling. She was left with a scar that runs inside the bridge of her nose. It was only later that my mother told me there had been a few nights when I was away on vacation that the doctors had told my parents she could lose her eye and that dying from the infection was not impossible. Without insurance, they paid off Theresa's hospital bills over the next several years. Their debts and stresses mounted.

———————

A few days after Orville, I'm standing in a dead woman's bedroom with a retired cop named George. We're putting on our rubber gloves when a guy we hadn't yet seen in the house comes storming down the hall toward us gripping a pair of long scissors like a knife. He's wiry and short with long, lank hair and a mustache. His left eye's a different shape from the right. The first word that forms in my head is "Manson." His face is red, his mouth open as he comes at us. I assume that the removal of this woman's body has deranged him. In these seconds I try to gauge whether he'll stab us before we can wrestle the scissors away.

But in his manic frenzy Manson moves past us and vaults himself up on the bed. He straddles the dead woman. He clips a few locks of her hair, whispers to her. He bounces off the bed and stalks away without ever having looked at us.

Afterward in the hearse I say, "I thought he was going to kill us."

George says, "I'd kill you, too, if I thought you were there to hurt my mother."

I don't say anything. Just think about my mom, who lives with so much pain and silence. I'd like to think I'd stab someone who hurt her, but I've never said word one to my father about anything.

"Anyway," George says, "as soon as I saw that bastard coming down the hall I had my hand on my gun."

I can tell George knows what I'm thinking. You're carrying a gun? He's a gentle-seeming guy who's been urging me to go back to college. He brags about his son—"not much older than you," he says—graduating soon from medical school.

George keeps his eyes on the road. He says, "This is Frankford, son."

———

A little more than a year after Dad was fired I'm walking home from school one day when I see my neighbor Richie Hollins. We're juniors. He gets out after seventh period. I get out after eighth. He's already changed clothes and is heading back out. He tells me he expects to get jumped today. The girl he's seeing, her ex isn't happy about her being with Richie. Her ex is a lanky, goofy kid who'd been a few years ahead of us in school. Richie lifts his pant leg and shows me an ankle-holstered pistol.

That night I'm watching *Homefront*, a show about World War II soldiers newly returned from battle. At one of the commercial breaks, a tease for the local eleven o'clock news shows

Richie, hands cuffed behind his back, stepping up into the back of a paddy wagon.

Jumped by the goofy kid shot the goofy kid dead shot the goofy kid's friend.

For several days after that I just stare at my teachers without hearing them. I stare at my homework without lifting a pen. My history teacher knows I've grown up with Richie, sees I'm in a fog. He sends me to the school's guidance counselor, who says, "Do you think maybe you're upset because you're putting yourself in Richie's shoes? Are you projecting, Andy?" I have no idea what he means, only that he's implying my shutting down is somehow my fault. I do know that other than the current spell of not being able to read or write, it doesn't feel like I'm upset at all. I never feel close to tears. But my outsides have become even more frozen than before, and the tiny remnant of who I was before the house went silent has retreated even deeper inside the command center. This counselor is the first adult I've talked to intimately since my dad was fired, but he only asks questions about Richie Hollins. I don't like him or trust him enough to say anything else.

3

"Andy, get me a bucket," my father calls up from the cellar. "Jesus fucking Christ," he says. He's not usually an F-bomber. It's Memorial Day, 1993, the day before my last week of high school. I am seventeen. He's forty-five. He's gained a paunch, and it's taken him a while but he's grown a full beard. One day in this era we're driving together and another driver at an intersection waves us through a stop sign and yells as we pass, "Hey! Steven Spielberg!" When I hand him the empty bucket, Dad says, "Empty the Shop-Vac, will ya?" He's bent over picking file folders full of drafts of old poems out of the muck. "Ah, Christ," he says at the discovery of a fresh ruin. The iron soil pipe, three years shy of its ninetieth birthday, has caved in to old age. Six inches across, exposed, its outside a deep rusty brown and rough as stucco, it runs the length of the cellar wall from the back of the house to the front and out through the wall of Dad's office to the curb, where it meets the city sewer system. Cracks in the soil pipe have caused minor floods down here the past few years, but today he's come down to discover it crumbled, leaving the cellar an inch deep in wastewater. He keeps books and old records down here. Mom's sewing machine and her fabrics are here. Theresa's and my old toys are in boxes, among other boxes of china and silverware and glassware. Old tax returns. Christmas decorations. We walk the buckets upstairs, out through the kitchen, dump them on the grass in the back-yard. My sister comes down to help, and then my mother.

The muscles in my chest tighten when Mom starts down the steps. She's forty-four, growing heavy and gray, too. When he's around she closes herself behind a wall. She's building a convent back there, no suitors allowed. There's a school behind the wall, and a church. I'm always uncomfortable being in the same room with the both of them, but when something's gone wrong—if the car breaks down or an issue with the house like this—it's worse. It makes me feel for my father, and sympathy does not run easily from me to him in these days. Usually when he's around I'm an ornery, passive-aggressive little fucker. I didn't talk to him for a month or two after he was fired, and after that instead of Dad I started calling him Big Guy. He never said a word about it, just abided a fool's condescension. But in this case it feels comical how rotten this is, shit in all his private files. No one deserves this. And to present the woman you've so severely disappointed with this latest misery seems beyond what anyone should have to take.

The four of us work through the swampy late afternoon and evening, into the night, sweat dripping off our noses, jostling each other in close quarters but not talking, hot skin on skin with no eye contact, bailing buckets of our brown slop and toilet paper turned to white jelly.

One part depression, this scene: life is miserable now; it's inevitable, inescapable; how would we even begin to fight it? We're knee-deep in shit.

And one part naïveté: things aren't so bad; nobody died, right; we're all together.

A few days later, a plumber, so he can replace the soil pipe, has a backhoe come and dig out the hedges and the ivy in front of our house. For years after this, nothing green grows. My mother plants new hedges, but they don't take. We are the house on the block with a dirt patch out front.

In the hallway between my parents' bedroom and mine was a narrow walk-in closet that held linens and towels and winter coats, and it was where the attic could be accessed by a splintery wooden ladder as old as the house. One day deep in the back, my body pressed between the ladder and a stack of folded sheets—I was maybe ten, bored, it was summer—I rifled my parents' toiletry bag. Q-tips, travel toothbrushes, hotel shampoo, a small bottle of Sea Breeze for mosquito bites. Nothing new. I unzipped the last of a series of side pockets on a final stab at titillation, and there found a single Trojan condom. I remember thinking that I should be disgusted, as this seemed to be the common reaction by kids I knew at any hint of sexual affection between their parents, but I felt overcome by something like a deep reassurance.

———————

This is when my idiocy started to pile up.

In the middle years of high school I scored well enough on standardized tests that I got mail from colleges all over the country, places like UCLA and Northwestern and Miami. Enough came to fill cardboard boxes that took up almost all the space under my bed. I was sleeping on a pile of tickets out of a house where no one spoke, out of a neighborhood where no one wanted to be, out of a city that hated itself more than I did. Of course one school was forbidden by good sense, one I couldn't consider attending. How could I consider it? Why would I? Only one college among the thousands in North America was a choice that logic said I must banish, because it was the place that had banished my father, and it was the place where he betrayed the family, and it was a place of happy memories gone bitter.

But idiots are predictable, and there was a feeling of inevitability about my going to La Salle. When he was fired, my father had made a deal that said, You can fire me, but my kids will get free tuition. I won a partial scholarship to Fordham's campus at Lincoln Center in Manhattan, but the remainder was out of my parents' range. I'd dreamed in high school of going to Northwestern or Syracuse for sportswriting, but their applications asked for essays I never got around to writing.

I got a call the spring of senior year from the head of La Salle's Honors Program. He talked to me a few minutes, told me I'd won a full scholarship. Apparently this guy had no idea who I was. He told me a little about what I should expect if I chose La Salle, how much of an advantage I'd have by taking Honors classes, and so on. I felt such relief from the thought that not only had I won a full scholarship but it was based on anonymous merit. I thanked him and we said our good-byes. As we were hanging up he said, "Oh, Andy, tell your dad I said hi."

I had it in my head I would go to La Salle to redeem my father. More than that, I figured I'd have a super time, graduate with great grades. These are an idiot's thoughts, the same kind I'd had before I started high school, where on the first day of freshman year, on a tour of the basketball gym, I'd pictured myself in the bleachers as a senior with my steady girlfriend as played by Elisabeth Shue. In fact on the night of my senior prom I asked off from the deli where I worked and went to a Flyers game with one of the guys I made hoagies with.

There was a part of me, too, that wanted to go to La Salle to stick it to my father. You know who can succeed at the place that shitcanned you? I can. You know who's welcomed there, Big Guy? I am.

One Saturday night Mom called upstairs to me. I was twenty-two. "Your father's on the phone," she said. It had been eight years since she'd called him Dad. Now he was always Your

Father. I went into their bedroom and picked up the extension. "Hey, buddy," he said. "I'm over here at JFK. They sent me alone, but the woman's five hundred pounds."

I wanted to see.

"I don't know what time you're going out," he said, "but do you think you could come over here? If they don't want to pay you, I will."

The hospital was in Summerdale, a neighborhood of cops and firemen just across Roosevelt Boulevard from Frankford. When I got there Dad was waiting by the hearse. Clean shaven, he wore his white shirt, black tie, black pants and loafers, but on this night instead of a black suit jacket and topcoat he wore a gray cashmere sweater under a slick black leather blazer. He looked like a tony Gallic hit man sent to kill Yves Montand. I watched so many movies in those days my brain was constantly casting. On this night I'd say get me Alain Delon for Dad. If not, maybe Gary Oldman. He had already rolled the stretcher in, so we walked together, unencumbered, through the hospital basement to the morgue. "Nice place, huh?" he said as we strolled.

The basements of hospitals are underlit labyrinths of hallways garlanded with exposed ventilation pipes, littered with landmarks that help you remember the way back to the loading dock: industrial-size rolling hampers, empty gurneys, red-bagged trash cans for hazardous waste. They're loud from power generators and monolithic air-conditioning units and from workers, hidden away from patients, who don't have to modulate like their aboveground peers. The kitchen is always the loudest part, with big dishwashers running, glasses and silverware jangling, a woman in a hairnet seen through the circular window of a two-way door yelling to a colleague out of sight, "Yo, where JoJo at?" The hallway past the kitchen smells like Pine-Sol and dishwasher steam and two hundred portions of microwaved brown gravy. In many hospital basements the kitchen and morgue share the same stretch of hall. This tells you enough about hospitals. A security guard waited at the end of the hallway.

The morgue, like most, was a two-room suite: an anteroom, where the body could be wrapped in plastic by an orderly or identified by a funeral director, and, adjacent, a walk-in refrigerator, where the bodies keep. In the anteroom Dad signed a logbook saying which funeral home he represented, what time he'd been there, and the name of the deceased, which on this night was Susan. Once he'd signed, the guard gave him the death certificate, which Dad tucked under the Reeves. The guard then opened the cold-box door. Susan's body, wrapped in white plastic, loomed, at its highest point, near her middle, at least three feet above the stainless-steel rolling table she lay upon. Widthwise, she took up all of it, which was broader by half than our stretcher.

"Just get the feet over first," Dad said. "Okay? This is always the way."

A feat of engineering, I would start to learn that night, getting an obese case from her morgue table onto the stretcher. With someone so heavy, pulling a single foot over is a start, but in a hospital usually the body's already in a white plastic body bag or wrapped in white plastic sheets and taped up, as she was. Most hospital bodies, it's true, look like person-size sperm, but Susan was, I'm afraid, a Guinness Book, Ripley's Believe It or Not!, Texas State Fair–winning, five-hundred-pound jizz load. She was two Eagles linebackers in a trash bag.

———————

I started at La Salle when I was seventeen, in September 1993, three years after my father had been fired. On the first day of a religion class, the teacher, a white-haired, well-fed Christian Brother whom I'd never met, never even seen before, read everyone's name on the roll and waited for a "Here." When he got to the space where my name should've been called, he didn't say anything, just nodded without looking up, mouthed the word "Meredith," and made a check before calling the next name. Maybe he had liked my dad and would've liked me, maybe he would've even hooked me up with a better grade than I deserved, but I didn't go back to his class after that first day. I wanted only to be anonymous. I wanted no association with my father, which was a stretch since I had enrolled at the school where he'd spent twenty years and was fired in a scandal. There was no voice in me that felt like a reliable advocate for my well-being. I had no ability to muster the grit and planning I needed to put myself in a better situation. And from the first day there I experienced a sensation that never left me: that I was Shaggy walking down a hallway in an episode of *Scooby-Doo*, with the eyes of the portraits following me. None of my classmates knew that I'd been on this campus since I was born, that I'd gone to nursery school here, been to my mother's college graduation here, been to too many basketball games to count, seen the school plays, come to the open house every year, eaten on the fake Eames chairs in the cafeteria, that I knew the old women in the mail room, had played racquetball in the gym with my dad, had run up and down the hills on the quad, hills which now, to a six-foot-one seventeen-year-old, felt alarmingly small. Teachers in the English department had known me since I was born. If my dad had still taught at La Salle, untainted, and I had gone there, I would've dealt with the weight of being his son, too. Maybe teachers would've eyed me, would've expected me to be a certain way. But it was a unique weight, him having been fired. The teachers all knew something very private about me, they knew the red mark on my family. No one in my high school would have known about it except one friend whose sister was enrolled at La Salle at the time, and he had never said a word to me. My other friends wouldn't have known unless I had told them, and I hadn't. But my teachers at La Salle knew. Being there meant an extra weight, an unnecessary and stupid one.

———

Nearly every ministration involved in moving a five-hundred-pound body starts with the words "Okay. One, two, three." We were standing alongside the stretcher, reaching across its empty width, the tops of our thighs holding it in place. Dad put both his hands on her far calf. I cupped one hand under each of her heels. Dad said, "Okay. One, two, three, pull," the last word trailing off in a grunt. Even with the security guard pushing from the opposite side, after a ten-second spurting of red-faced jerks we had hardly budged her. Only her feet, not even her ankles, made it over to the stretcher. Ninety-nine percent of her weight remained unmoved. We tried again.

"One, two, three, pull," Dad said again. Nothing. "Jesus Christ." Then he asked the guard, "You have anybody else who could help us?"

The guard: "Nope. I'm it."

Dad let his head slump to one side in outsize exasperation. A breath leaked out between his lips.

"Maybe we could saw her in half," I said.

Dad said to the guard, "Can I use the phone?" He pulled out his beeper for the number and called the funeral director. "Hi, Gene. I'm at the hospital. Did the family tell you anything about the body? No? She's a big one. She's five hundred pounds. Yeah. Five hundred. I called my son. He's here. And we have a guard helping. We can't move her. You have anybody else who could come? I know it's Saturday night. Okay. Thanks, Gene. Beep me if you need me. Thanks." He hung up. "Gene's sending two more guys."

"How did she let it get so bad?" I said. "Five guys just because she couldn't stop eating." I was fascinated by how powerless she must've felt. That's when you really understand that the self is not a single entity, when one part feels constant dread at what the other keeps doing, at how much pain the impulsive self visits on the observant one.

"Let's go wait outside," Dad said to me.

"She's imposing on people," I said. I had become a fanatic about imposition. "Even in death."

A half dozen streets die at the east side of JFK Hospital. Standing on the loading dock we could see the brick walls of the ends of these rows of two-story homes.

"Ever think we'd be doing this?" I said.

"Hauling bodies?" My father looked up at the sky. "No."

Here was an opening for a question like "Then how did you picture us turning out?" Maybe I needed to say "One two three" to get the real weight in our lives moving. Instead I said, "I guess it's not the worst thing in the world."

It was these kinds of moments that were our family specialty. We spent so much time within five feet of each other—none of us ever went anywhere—and yet every sitting at the dinner table together, every ride to the Acme together, nearly any and every opportunity to talk about something deeper than sports and the weather and the pertinent details of the day, anything deeper than "What time do you need to be picked up?" we defused.

Two other guys showed up, and it took the four of us plus whatever effort the security guard contributed to get this woman over. She was half again wider than the stretcher, so moving her out of the morgue and down the hall meant gripping fat and going slow. We got her out onto the loading dock, and then slowly down the ramp, with four of us backing down alongside and ahead of her, with Dad steering at the head end. Next we got the foot end of the stretcher up over the hearse's back-door lip.

There's a moment when the remover has to squeeze the two

handles in the stretcher's undercarriage to release the wheeled legs, leaving nearly all the deceased's weight in his hands. With a one-hundred-pound body this means a nearly imperceptible exertion, an unremarkable moment. A two-hundred-pounder, I would come to learn, elicits a grunt and a mild strain in the face that lasts less than a second before the momentum of the back wheels sliding into the hearse takes over. With a two-hundred-and-fifty-pounder the remover might let some of the weight rest on the tops of his thighs. By three hundred pounds, he wants help. He might not get it or need it necessarily, but it's probably best to have someone there, a spotter, to avoid tipping, or in case of some kind of failure of his muscles or the stretcher's legs. A five-hundred-pound body, like Susan's, demands a team: extra hands for stability and extra muscle for that moment when all the weight belongs to the removers. On this night, Dad was in charge of the head-end weight. He counted "One, two, three" again at the moment he was going to release the legs. The other four of us stood two on each side of the stretcher, holding it like we would to slide a casket into the hearse. When he released the legs there was a second before the forward momentum of her slide into the dark car began, when the five of us shared the five hundred pounds, but Dad, standing at Susan's head, held the most weight, and he was the one with the best leverage for driving her forward. He exhaled coolly, and put her away.

Once she was in, there was a laugh of relief that even the security guard shared. The four of us then drove to the funeral home in our separate cars. We got Susan up the ramp into the morgue, then had to finagle four heavy nylon straps under her body. Once this was done we hooked the straps to a hydraulic hoist mounted in one of the ceiling beams. Now she was out of our hands. I remember the whine of the hoist's motor like the compactor on a trash truck, the men's slightly pursed lips, the slow tightening of the straps against the underside of this giant white marshmallow. And then she was in flight. For maybe thirty seconds as she was lifted off her stretcher and lowered onto the embalming table Susan arced through the air of the morgue with the four of us standing around her like moons.

My first year at La Salle I lived on campus. I didn't drink, I was terrible at talking to girls, and the more I saw my hallmates enjoying themselves the more I felt alone. I hated being there, but of course I hated everything. I was depressed, without knowing it or even knowing what depression was. I just thought this was how I was turning out, that this hollow gloom I walked around in was meant to be my life.

One day at lunch in the cafeteria in the first month of school, an older girl, a junior named Valerie, came and sat next to me. I had never seen her before. She was nineteen. I was seventeen. She was tiny, with long black curly hair and too much black eyeliner. Immediately I could feel that we walked under the same gray skies. She told me she had a boyfriend, so I thought her talking to a strange male like myself was unusual. He went to La Salle, too, she said, but he commuted. The next day I saw her walking with him on campus—she saw me but ignored me—so I knew who he was.

It sounds like the move of someone equipped with boldness to start seeing an older girl with a boyfriend. It wasn't. She said she'd been noticing me. She invited me to her room. I had no idea what would happen, but I had enough sense to show up. As soon as I got there she started kissing me and let me take her shirt off. I left mine on because I hated my body. If you had asked me at seventeen to draw a picture of my self-image, I would have traced a photograph of the teenage Jerry Mathers, somehow gangly and pudgy at the same time, like a skeleton smuggling kielbasa under his sweater.

After that first day with her it became a regular thing. I would go to her room and we'd make out. Her boyfriend would call and I'd lie there rigid and silent as she told him, "No, there's no one here." After a few sessions it became the norm that she would let me put my fingers inside her. When it was done she would cry. This went on for a few weeks. One day in the courtyard between our dorms I saw her talking to a guy I had a class with. A few days later I saw her talking to another guy. The invitations to her room dwindled.

The Phillies blew the World Series on a Saturday night, and the next morning in despair I asked a kid in my hallway to shave my head. I had no room for the luxury of hair. When she saw me later that day she said, "Any attraction I had to you is gone."

One night after Christmas break she came to my room and said she wanted to talk. We sat side by side on the bed. She rubbed my thigh, tried to kiss me. I said I wasn't interested. At the door she said, "I want you to know I only used you. I never liked you."

"That's fine," I said.

"Do you understand? I never liked you. I used you."

———

I moved home after freshman year, returned to what I knew. One of my first days back in Frankford I was walking on Orthodox Street past the park in the late afternoon and in my peripheral vision I saw a man sitting under a weeping willow, his back against the trunk, and noted someone else huddled next to him. I turned my head to them. I saw, under the willow's shady canopy, a woman taking the man's penis in her mouth, an act I had never before in any form witnessed. I turned to look straight ahead down Orthodox Street. I snapped my head back to them and saw again a woman giving a man a blow job under a weeping willow, her hand gripping his penis while she disengaged to tuck back her hair; his eyes closing and staying shut; she resuming.

———

Until I was ten, our next-door neighbor was a woman named Eleanor Hippel. In 1906, Miss Hippel was born in the house where she lived her whole life, 4627 Oakland Street. She had already lived in her house seventy years when my parents moved into 4625 Oakland in December 1976, when I was one. If you said to me, "Describe the average seventy-five-year-old woman living in Frankford in the early 1980s," I'd provide you with a whole list of suppositions: she's a widow; she wears cat's-eye glasses; she spends a chunk of every morning sweeping her front steps with a kitchen broom; she wears a housedress and rolled-down stockings and pulls a silver shopping cart home from the grocery store; she ties a flower-print kerchief under her chin to cover her head on cold days and on rainy days she protects her hair with a sheet of clear plastic. What I didn't get as a kid was that these were Old World women. They might have been born in Philadelphia, their parents might even have been, but their style of living, for reasons having mostly to do with social class and education, hadn't changed much since Sicily or Warsaw or County Clare.

In a part of the city with a Catholic church seemingly on every other block, Miss Hippel was an Episcopalian. Her father had been an executive with the Philadelphia Electric Company, PECO, and had bought his new home when Frankford was about as far out as you could live and still make it to an office in Center City. (The elevated train wouldn't connect Frankford with downtown until 1922, so I'm guessing Mr. Hippel either commuted by trolley or was a very early adopter of the automobile.) Miss Hippel spent most of her adult life as a secretary at PECO. She retired to play golf and tennis, and she looked the part: tall and slim, curly blond hair, a golden tan, slacks and cashmere sweaters in winter, plaid shorts and golf shirts or white tennis dresses in summer. She had never married, but even in her seventies she was pretty and ebullient. She would talk with such joy about the time she met Arnold

Palmer, her decades-long crush. She smoked Virginia Slims. She had a friend named Sheree (shuh-REE), whom she'd grown up with in Frankford. Sheree lived in Monterey and when she visited in the summers would bring my parents a loaf of sourdough bread from San Francisco.

Miss Hippel was kind, an eager babysitter, and had that bygone romance about her that my parents, more than any other neighbors, were helpless against. My dad especially liked her. Unlike my mother, she drank a bit and smoked. In summer the three of them would sit behind the houses at cocktail hour, the yards separated only by a two-foot-high wall of stacked bricks that they would put their feet up on. Miss Hippel knew the history of the neighborhood, the block, and our house, which especially fascinated my father. She loved to tell us that when she was a little girl there were no houses on the other side of Oakland Street, just meadow, with sheep grazing by a stream. By the early eighties you'd have to drive maybe thirty miles outside the city to see a sheep, but she kept a touch of that wilderness alive. The backyards on our block were a uniform size, about thirty feet deep and twelve feet wide. Miss Hippel's was something different: a brick path crowded on both sides by explosions of snowdrops, daisies, ferns, azaleas, cosmos, violets, dusty miller, mums. Her front yard, maybe fifteen by ten, was covered in pachysandra and surrounded by a regal chest-high hedge. (We had the same kind of hedge in front of our house, only with ivy as ground cover. In spring, somehow, a few daffodils would come up through Miss Hippel's pachysandra but never through our ivy.) My father has a poem called "Hippel's Wilderness" that says a lot of what I'm trying to say, but much better. One stanza reads:

You have seen the faces fall away, like trees
along the street, and, grey, the soot from diesels
build up everywhere, traffic rattling
sashes up and down the block. But you
have saved a bit of city as it was.
In a yard smaller than a good-sized truck
Frankford as it used to be goes on.

Our house shared an enclosed porch with Miss Hippel's. Between the two porches was a window that swung open. (It had been painted shut for decades, but my father chiseled the paint away one day to make the commerce between houses easier, and so that on winter nights she could come in or vice versa without having to set foot on icy steps and sidewalk.) Many Saturdays in fall and winter the four Merediths would climb through to her house for cocktail hour. One night I wore a blazer over my usual T-shirt and sweatpants, and Dad tied me a bow tie. Theresa and I drank orange juice in highball glasses. I remember, too, handfuls of macadamia nuts; the smell of cigarettes rich in the butterscotch carpet; easy laughs among the adults; golf from the West Coast on the television in the early dark of winter. Miss Hippel was like a third grandmother to my sister and me, but she did so many things our parents' mothers never did. She traveled, had a career, played sports, lived alone. Neither of our parents' mothers drove, but Miss

Hippel kept her cream-colored '66 Buick Skylark convertible in a garage in the neighborhood and would take it out to the Main Line to play golf or visit a nephew or her old friends, human links to a time when it was not inconceivable to leave Frankford for enclaves like Bryn Mawr or Swarthmore. No one else I've met in my life has left Frankford for Bryn Mawr or Swarthmore.

In 1985, Miss Hippel gave up her Skylark after an accident, and my mom started to shop for her groceries. Later in the year she moved out to the Main Line to live in a nursing home near her nephew and his family. She died in the spring of 1986.

Her house wasn't empty for long. By the summer a couple named Peg and Bill Stanley moved in with their three toddlers. The day they arrived they backed a pickup truck full of their possessions over Miss Hippel's hedges. After moving day they dug out the remaining hedges and pachysandra. In its place they threw down grass seed that never held for all their kids' foot traffic. The Stanleys eventually bought a Rottweiler named Tank that would sit in their front window and, seemingly as if trained, bark in long, lingering rumbles whenever a black person walked by. One day Tank was reduced to cowering by an aggressive poodle on the block. For the rest of that night we could hear Bill through the wall bellowing about his "faggot dog." "Buy a rockweiler and he's scared of a fuckin' poodle. You're a fuckin' faggot dog." Before the summer was over all of Miss Hippel's backyard flora was gone, replaced by a monster aboveground swimming pool. Peg and Bill and their friends would stay out there till late at night drinking beers and smoking joints. The four of us spent more time inside than ever.

By Christmas of 1986, Miss Hippel, both of my dad's parents, and our neighbor Mrs. Hollins, who was my mom's close friend and the mother of my buddy, Richie, had all died in a twelve-month span. Mom stood on the front porch that day and cried about the hedge. She cried the rest of that night. Grief, I'm sure, but also the fear of trading one kind of wilderness for another.

———

I'm a sophomore at La Salle. A Sunday morning, fall of 1994, at home. My dad and I have squeezed out the attic window—maybe eighteen inches high—onto the sooty roof. When we stand up we're black-bellied chimney sweeps. From here we can see maybe the top three or four stories of a brick building we call the Sears Tower, about a mile from our house. Sears, Roebuck warehouse space beneath a square, nine-story clock tower full of offices—my dad's mother worked there for a time—it was the tallest building in Northeast Philadelphia, our little Big Ben. The great landmark of our part of the world, this monument to Frankford's early-twentieth-century economic health can be seen from downtown high-rises seven miles away, and from the nearby bridges to New Jersey.

From our roof it's a giant brown owl watching over Frankford. Before we hear the blast, we see the tower list slightly right. There is an instant when the tower doesn't move any farther, and I have a flash of hope that the implosion has failed, that we—the neighborhood, my father and I—have lucked into a reprieve, or a time warp. When the tower drops out of sight, Dad mutters, "Bastards." Great clouds of milk-colored particulate rise up in its place.

The factories had all closed in his lifetime. The railroads were dead, the trestles removed. Longtime neighbors were bolting for the suburbs. Now the Sears Tower was blown up.

————

I started flunking courses at La Salle in my sophomore year. In my fifth semester, after collecting roughly three semesters' worth of credits, I was asked to leave.

————

One afternoon in the summer of 1995 my mother and I sat at the kitchen table. For whatever reason—I don't remember what led me to this, because never did we speak so candidly—I said, "Are you depressed?" She looked at me plainly and said, "Yes." I pursed my lips. I didn't even nod. I said nothing more and neither did she. The question and its answer just sat at the table with us. And then I left the room.

I had inched toward some greater connection with her, toward being her real friend, but I shied away from the potential energy. Maybe it wasn't my job to be her friend. Maybe she should've gone to therapy or asked for a scrip for antidepressants, but these are rationalizations formed after the fact. We had all retreated too far into ourselves to be available for human interactions, and for that one moment when maybe we were both available, both ready, both up at the surface, I dove back underwater at the first sign of land. Deep under. All four of us. We lived in bathyspheres, but of course we didn't want to.

A few weeks before that, my dad's side of the family had caravanned from Philadelphia to Pittsburgh for my cousin's wedding. My mother didn't go. Her mother was sick, but I'm sure she would've gone with us if things with my father had been different. I don't know what she knew about his personal life in that time, but he seemed to be, if not actively carrying on a robust sex life, then at least acting like someone who wanted to be. At the wedding one of my cousins pointed out to me that my father was wearing his claddagh ring with the heart facing out, which apparently meant he was looking for love.

Whereas my dad seemed unable to stop himself from flirting with my sister's friends, female cashiers, female toll takers, and female funeral directors, I never saw my mother do or say anything to acknowledge attraction outside her marriage besides loyally tuning in to Peter Jennings's newscast. I don't know if I ever saw my parents share a kiss that transcended in duration or passion the kind of peck I would give my grandmother. The kisses they exchanged in front of us before my father's firing in 1990 were no less perfunctory-seeming than after, when they would sometimes be forced by circumstance— the gift of peace at the rare mass Dad would attend—to lean into each other. I don't ever remember seeing them hold hands or put an arm around the other's shoulder. When I was small, if my mother was having a bad day, sometimes she and my father would move into another room and exchange a long, weary hug. If I walked in, the hug would break up. As I got a little older I would know they were hugging because their talking would stop, and I would go to where they were because I wanted to see. This is my memory of their bodies touching.

I traveled to my cousin's wedding with the expired driver's license of a twenty-four-year-old guy I worked with. I got drunk with my cousins and aunts and uncles in the hotel bar Friday night and then again Saturday after the wedding. There was a freedom in the drunkenness something like euphoria. Love and nostalgia were turned up, shyness was turned down; these few nights were the happiest I'd managed since puberty.

I spent part of both of these nights chatting up a bridesmaid whom, because of nerves, I was barely able to look at before a half dozen screwdrivers. Cute enough in the face, she was stupendously voluptuous, a quality enhanced by her strapless gown. At one point, after a conversation with her—presumably a talk at least partly about Pavement; I was too drunk to remember—had gone well, I asked my cousin Johnny if I could borrow a condom, which was presumptuous for a virgin but, in fairness, not so off base.

She and I left the hotel bar at the closing hour, and I led us out into the parking lot. Unbeknownst to me, Dad, who'd been talking to the both of us, followed. I dimly assumed he'd read my intentions and would let us alone. We got to a place where all the exiting cousins and aunts and uncles had drifted away, leaving just the three of us. We talked for a bit, and then there was a silence in which it struck me that my father and I were waiting to see who would leave first.

I resolved not to say a word until he did. I remember looking at him and him looking at me from behind that face I'd seen nearly every day of my life: his brown eyes and wire-framed glasses, his long nose, his thin upper lip covered with a mustache. The face of life. What else does a son think about his father's face? It's almost embarrassing to look at it too long, the face of your creator.

I was looking down now, biting my lower lip. I don't know what the bridesmaid thought. I couldn't look at her. Finally he said, "Okay," like he was granting me a favor, and said good night. I don't think he was angry with me. Maybe frustrated. Or maybe he wasn't trying for her at all. It seemed like it, certainly. But maybe I had it wrong. I was drunk enough for that to be true. After he left I couldn't say two coherent words to the girl—I was drunk, yes, but had been talking just fine before; *spells had been cast and the urge had been lost*—and after a minute of no words or eye contact, she shook my hand and went to her room. When she left I sat at the bottom of the steps leading up to the second deck of rooms. I'd shifted from a few-days-long stretch of feeling free, buoyed, hopeful to weighed down heavier than I could ever remember. At nineteen I was still lost in the shelter and damage of my adolescence.

That same summer, on a drive with my mother along Snake Road (just using it as a shortcut, not as its own destination; those days were gone), she said, "Do you want to know what he did?" She was angry at me, I think for having complimented my father about something. They were still living together, so no matter what she told me she was still going to share his bed that night.

"Do you want to know what he was fired for?" she said.

"No," I said.

———

Six months after the Pittsburgh wedding, a few weeks after being kicked out of La Salle College for good, I got a job through a friend doing data entry for Blue Cross Blue Shield in an office downtown. I did it for seven or eight months, and then I enrolled at Temple, where I lasted one semester before I flunked out. After that I got a job—through my cousin Shane, who also worked for Livery of Frankford—as a busboy in a sandwich shop downtown. I worked there seven or eight months and then went back to Temple and flunked out again. In this same time frame, my sister graduated from high school and started at Penn. When she enrolled, my dad took a second job to help pay for her tuition. This was when he was hired— through Shane—by Livery of Frankford.

4

One warm Saturday night in October 1995—I was nineteen, in my last semester at La Salle—I went out with Gazz; his girlfriend, Kelly; and a pack of the guys Gazz had grown up with, to a punishingly loud club in West Philadelphia called FUBAR. Gazz's buddies, sweet and tender hooligans, found fistfights every other time they went out, and their idea of fun was to wait for one of their cohort to pass out drunk and set his feet on fire. Choochie, Bopper, Bob-o, Dom 1, Dom 2, Schroeder, Pooj, there were maybe a dozen and a half of these guys, and they had all grown up within a few blocks of each other in Port Richmond. Most of their parents had grown up together, too. (They made me ache at the thought of how sparsely kid-populated my corner of Frankford had been.) Gazz was the only one of them who traveled with a friend from another neighborhood. For whatever reason—probably because I was harmless-seeming—they accepted me. Still, they must've thought the two of us were weird. I was long and goofy, big ears hands feet, skinny with the muscle tone of a newborn, a head taller than Gazz, who was fit and handsome with long, straight hair like Gram Parsons, and we spent most of our time whispering to each other.

In this era, going to a club like this—one aimed at attracting hordes of white kids with fake IDs—meant subjecting oneself to a never slackening dosage of Alanis Morissette, so we two spent the night conferring, huddled so as to defend the nobler flame of our culture, swallowing large amounts of bitter Yuengling Porter, as was the custom, while mixing in occasional shots that were thrust toward our faces by friends: kamikazes, Alabama slammers, lemon drops, and straight-up doses of Jägermeister and Goldschläger.

"*Green*—listen. *Green* is not better than *Reckoning*. It's not. Let me just say that, because that just—that just feels important to say out loud."

"Here's a question. For you. Does *Reckoning* have 'Hairshirt'?"

"Does *Green* have 'Harborcoat'?"

"'*I am not the type of dog.*'"

"The real killer—you know what the real killer is."

"Tell me."

"Is 'World Leader Pretend.'"

"'*I sit at my table.*'"

"'*Seems like it's all, it's all for nothing.*'"

"The one song on that record, though, you know what it is, the one we'll be listening to in fifty years."

"Do you see that ass?"

"Talk to her."

"I need an ass like that."

"Go talk to her."

"Maybe in a minute I will."

"The one I want to hear when the lights are out and I'm in a fight with Kelly and nothing's making me feel better."

"Yup."

"The one that may or may not put a lump in my throat every time I hear it."

"I know."

"Say it."

"'You Are the Everything.'"

"We've talked about this a dozen times."

"Might be their best song. Period."

"Who am I to argue?"

"'*Drifting off to sleep / with your teeth in your mouth.*'"

For as much as I loved pop songs, for as strong as my yearning was for the intimacy of a human voice coming through headphones into my body, for as much as it was the only love I knew how to receive, a transfusion of tender sacred self setting my breastbone limp like ramen, Joni Mitchell making my shins go cold, the harmony in the Beach Boys' "Meant for You" rolling bumps up the back of my neck (and in the harmony, or maybe simply in the effort to harmonize, the suggestion of communion between the Wilson boys, as if this were the prerequisite: before a woman, first you must love your brothers), however music helped nourish my heart in these days when my home life was breaking it, however much it tried to instruct me in the sensual responsiveness of my body, however much I loved music and needed it, Gazz loved it and needed it more. His little brother was not coming back. At least my parents, ghosts that they'd become, walked among us. He was electrified with an underground sadness soothed only with the right songs. He was my teacher.

———

There were other teachers, too.

"Get the fuck in, get the fuck out. Ya got me? Get the fuck in, get the fuck out. That's the whole secret." This is Vince Visco—swarthy, overfed, sideburned, bald—a slightly taller Danny DeVito, the retired cop I'm out with on an afternoon removal. He's sharing with me the whole secret and I'm too dumb to hear it. My dad has trained me to park the hearse in front of the house and let one of the two men go in to greet the family and reconnoiter. Courteous and practical. This was how the other men did it, too. Vince Visco, though, doesn't want to waste a second. He figures the stop-and-chat adds precious minutes to the denominator of his imagined hourly rate. There is no hourly rate; we get thirty-five dollars whether it takes us ten minutes or three hours.

We're in a neighborhood in the Northeast called Fox Chase, a bastion for white-flighters who've left places like Kensington and Frankford but still need to live within the city limits to keep their jobs as cops and firemen. When I stay seated after I park the hearse he says, without looking at me because he's expected this moment, "Come on. Get out." He drags the stretcher behind him to the front door. I run a few steps to keep up. When a teenage boy answers the door, Vince says, "Where we goin'?" We're led into a bedroom on the first floor, where we're greeted by three middle-aged women. "We're her daughters," one of them says. I crinkle my eyes and, with my lips squeezed tight, nod at them. It's a look I've been developing. I want it to say, "I'm really glad to meet you. God, it's awful we're meeting like this over your dead mom. Good luck to you in everything. There's a decent chance I'll be parking your car at the funeral." I'm afraid, though, that, coupled with my suit and haircut, my look says, "I've been different since the war." Vince barely blinks at them before he's wrapping the woman in her bed-sheet. I look to see if the daughters are upset, but they seem giddy, something I've never seen before in my short career. Vince is in such an addled rush that some faint pulse of guilt or better nature must patch itself through to his tongue. He stops just before he covers the dead woman's face. He eyes her, then turns to her daughters and says, "She looks like a real nice lady." With great solemnity they all nod thank you, but the act of playing serious and his use of the present tense make them delirious. One laughs despite herself, and then the others laugh at him, too. They're holding their hands to their mouths, trying to behave. Vince smiles belatedly, but I can tell he doesn't get it. He's rattled.

Back in the car, he says, "You see what happens? Why did I have to say something? You see what happens when you waste time?"

———————

Near the end of the night at FUBAR, Kelly, who liked me fine but I'm sure wanted me to monopolize less of Gazz's time on the phone, stopped a girl who was walking by and asked her if she thought I was cute. The girl, Karen, a petite thing with a Dorothy Hamill bowl cut, said something that I understood as "I guess." The gallon of alcohol in my stomach and the fact that I was witnessing this human verify that indeed I was not 100 percent hideous gave me the spurt I needed to make an approach. My opening question, as it was to all new acquaintances, was "Do you like Pavement?" By the time she had been caught up on the band's creation story, the order in which to consume their records, and the universality with which critics seemed to ignore the chance to discuss *Crooked Rain* as a concept album, it was closing time. She gave me her phone number.

We went out the following Saturday night to a bar called Sugar Mom's, very near to where Benjamin Franklin had lived. In his honor I did what I was used to and got stumbling drunk on pints of porter. That night we went back to her dorm room at a local art school. I insisted she play, on repeat, R.E.M.'s new single, "Tongue," a Stylistics-style makeout song in which Michael Stipe's narrator urges, "Don't leave that stuff all over me," which made it a perfect ode to condoms on this, the first night I would ever roll one on. (This was still a few years before my first removal, i.e., before rolling on a condom reminded me of the reflexive act of pulling on plastic gloves at the sight of a dead body.) Between the rubber and the ten beers gulped at nervous speed, I didn't feel much when she put me inside her. The sensation was markedly less enthralling than the pleasure my own lotiony hand could summon on a slow Tuesday afternoon. I plugged away for a long time, maybe twenty minutes of straight-up missionary jackhammering. If I had been asked for a summary of the thousands of whizzing thoughts and observations from those twenty minutes, it would have been "Oh my god. There's a person stuck to my penis." How shattering to discover that sex with a partner was as much of a slog as the rest of adult life. Karen was alternating between closing her eyes tight and making sounds with her mouth, but I couldn't believe she was enjoying herself. Philadelphians are sandwich lovers nonpareil, but when I found myself, suspended on elbows over my first naked girl, conjuring a corned beef and Swiss shortie with mayo and pickles, I decided to ditch the mission. Hoagie interruptus. I offered several maximo bravado pumps and closed, like Monica Seles pouncing on a forehand, with a whopper of a grunt before stopping dead and setting on top of her like the flabby, long-limbed corpse I was. "You're finished?" she said. Indeed I was, but I left wondering about the technical requirements for losing one's flower.

We're on Bridge Street, Dad and I, at the last house west of I-95, the monolithic interstate highway whose arrival in the sixties ruptured the city's river wards. It's a tiny place made tinier by the roaring cars and trucks overhead. Dad goes in first. He comes out and says, "Yeesh." He widens his eyes. "It's gonna be tight." Inside, in an easy chair the color of pea soup, a dead man waits for us. Buzz cut, ample jowls, navy blue and red plaid flannel shirt open over a white undershirt, navy blue polyester slacks, thick through the chest. He reminds me of Dolph Sweet, who played the father on *Gimme a Break!* He looks like the kind of guy who was picking butts out of the gutter and smoking them when he was eight years old, like my dad's father had done. It doesn't hit me that in scruffy old men like this Dad must see Pop. We're only a mile or so from where he had lived. I remember him on a typical summer evening on his front porch, dressed in sleeveless undershirt; navy blue slacks, polyester; black dress socks. No bare feet. I think in all the nights of being in their homes, even counting the nights I slept over, I saw my four grandparents' bare feet a total of three times. I saw my mother's mother's feet for the first time the night before she died, when I helped lift her legs back into bed.

The next weekend I saw Karen again, and this time I was able to relax and enjoy the trip back to her room. She was twenty, a year older than I was, but tiny, nearly elfin, with a child's mini fingers and tender nails. She liked to talk hockey. One night I took her to a Friendly's near her campus; a young man's cache of seductive tricks must always include the Fribble. We ran out of things to talk about. The next week I was on the phone with her in my bedroom when I heard the doorbell ring downstairs. I was home alone. I asked her to hold on. It was a neighbor returning one of my mother's Pyrex dishes. On the way back into the living room I walked by the TV and saw the Sixers tipping off. I watched the whole game, forgetting about the phone. When I went back upstairs to use the bathroom I saw my bedroom light on, went in, and saw the phone sitting there off the hook. I picked it up and said, "Hello?" Karen said, "Hello? What happened?" I couldn't understand someone being so into talking to me that she would sit there for two hours with a silent phone to her ear. Yet I knew she really wasn't that interested in me. We barely knew each other. We didn't have any overwhelming rapport. We talked like strangers in Winnipeg. What kind of need, I wondered, would make a person hold a phone to her head for two hours? Whatever it was I wanted no part of it.

A few nights after that we went to my friend Bob's apartment for a soiree featuring five or six other young minds and a few cases of Old Milwaukee. Bob made Karen laugh, and even though she and I disappeared in the middle of the party to use his bedroom for sex, at the end of the night I told him he should ask her out. He told me I was crazy. I called her the next night and she said she couldn't talk because she had Bob on the other line. My response was to feel mortally wounded.

But something had changed. I had evidence of a girl liking me. For those few weeks of talking to Karen on the phone I hadn't felt so bad. And I had this taste of drama from it ending badly. I didn't know it at the time, but I was learning to use girls for the same sort of distraction from misery I used songs for. I started to get the idea that whatever was wrong with me, whatever it was that school hadn't solved, maybe girls would solve.

———

Pop Meredith's porch, like all the others on his block of row homes, was recessed about twenty feet from the curb, allowing room at the top of the first of two sets of steps for a landing that on most of the houses of the block was a concrete slab, but which my grandparents had converted to brick pavers with room enough for beds for tulips and marigolds, and for a rosebush that gave months of pink blooms. Pop watched cars go by, said hello to passing neighbors, tossed birdseed on the bricks. He cooed to the sparrows and chickadees that came to the porch's hanging feeder, and went still when one landed on the black wrought-iron railing in front of him, the creature eyeing him with seconds-hand ticks of its head. When it left, Pop ashed his Camel into the stand-up ashtray kept, indoors and out, always at his left hand, even though he was right-handed and needed to cross himself to ash. The ashtray stand was black plastic molded in the shape of a horse's head, an amber-colored glass dish resting on the crown of the skull. Granny sat next to him, working a needlepoint, and then talking with a neighbor who'd stopped by. A transistor radio was tuned to Harry Kalas and Whitey Ashburn calling the Phillies game. For all their charms, for the way their mutual affection came across in their chat, Harry and Whitey's pairing was made exquisite by its portions of silence. They felt no need to speak when the game didn't require it, and so they endowed the night with aching slips of quiet—five- and ten- and sometimes fifteen-second gaps—while the pitcher took his signs or called the catcher out for counsel. Many nights you could dial in the game not because you heard a play being reported but because you'd found the one spot on the dial where static gave way to a singular near absence of sound, no hiss, only the low, steady murmur of the crowd like a box fan running two rooms away.

Baseball on the radio, birds feeding, the porch's yellow smell of birdseed and tobacco, this is the scene my parents, my sister, and I would be received into on summer nights when we drove the five minutes from our house, down Oakland Street, crossing Arrott, Herbert, Foulkrod, Fillmore, Harrison, passing Frankford High School, where for one week in April the forsythia hedges would bloom yellow, crossing Allengrove, Wakeling, Oxford, Pratt, Bridge, making the left on Cheltenham up the hill to 1531. We were all couples then, single words: Grannyandpop, Marianandwill, Andrewandtheresa, Harryandwhitey. "Where are we going?" "To Grannyandpop's."

Dolph sits facing us with perfect posture, his back straight, feet on the floor, forearms on the arms of the chair, like a king receiving subjects. And here's why it's so tight: every inch of the palace is buried under old newspapers stacked in towers reaching higher than his head. All that's spared is a pathway as wide as a man. There must be rats, but we're lucky to miss them. Someone on this evening—a landlord? a nephew?—has let the paramedics in to pronounce the king dead but hasn't waited around for us. As we roll him out to the hearse, Dad says, "You don't see women die at home alone like this."

"What do you mean?" I say.

"Even if they're alone when they die, someone always turns out to see them off."

"But the men are different?"

"Seems like."

A few days after picking up the newspaper king I email my sister's friend Janie and ask her for a date. As with everything else, I don't see the cause and effect at the time.

———

Philadelphia, you big bitch, throw me a bone. It's June 1998. I'm twenty-two. I've bounced from failure at school to crappy job and back for two years. I spend my time outside the house either dragging the local dead around or getting drunk listening to rock and roll before coming chastely home to sleep ten feet down the hall from my parents. I've now handled far more dead women than live ones. I've only had sex a few times, only with one partner, and that was Karen, two and a half years ago.

———

At first Janie and I had been buddies. The summer before I started doing removals, I'd worked a temp job—through a friend—at Penn in their Center for Psychotherapy Research. Did they know how much research they could've done on me? A few times I saw an old, white-haired man in a bow tie walking the halls. The people who worked there, mostly psychology PhD students, whispered about him in awe. "That's Aaron Beck," they would say. I had no idea who he was, but they told me he'd invented the style of therapy practiced there. My job was to read transcripts of hour-long therapy sessions and write up one-page summaries. I noticed the therapists' mode of challenging the patients: "You say you can't talk to him, but why?" Pretty much my whole life was based on hang-ups and self-made obstacles that I'd never been pushed to defend or even acknowledge. Things like: of course I have to live with my parents; of course we can't talk about things; of course I should stay in Philadelphia. Reading other people's therapy sessions, responding to their therapists' prompts, I found myself in the best mood in years.

That summer, Janie worked at another office on Penn's campus. She had long blond hair, which wasn't my thing. I was looking for a Marisa Tomei stunt double. Janie wore modest sundresses and Birkenstocks, which also weren't my things. She was never not appropriately dressed for Lilith Fair. But she read *Anna Karenina* on the El through Kensington, which made her the only one doing that. And she looked at me through extraordinary violet eyes that triumphed over her hippie veneer. And after getting to know her, I saw that her clothes belied a glorious, sad edginess. She would laugh at the same blue material I could get Gazz with. We started a routine of meeting each day at noon on campus at a bench between a statue of Benjamin Franklin and a sculpture of a big broken button. I liked that she could talk for an hour with me barely adding a word—she had fire—but that she also listened when I had something to say. After a few of those lunches the talking balanced out between us, and we found we could get into just about anything and find ways to laugh. After we ate we'd walk around the neighborhood. She was nineteen. I was twenty-one. When the summer ended we were still just friends. She went back to her school in the Philadelphia suburbs, and I went back to Temple so I could drop out again.

That winter she came, at my sister's invitation, to my dad's fiftieth birthday party. My mom had organized the night; it would've looked funny if she hadn't, would've aroused suspicion about their union. So all my aunts and uncles came to our house, neighbors came, a few of my dad's friends, a few of his former students, and Janie, who was now a friend of both my sister and me.

There's a photo from that night of me posing with my arm around my mom. I'm smiling, eyelids half-closed from too many bottles of Yuengling. She's trying her best to smile, but because my father's the one taking the picture, her closed lips merely tighten and her cheek muscles gather around her eyes as if to defend them from the light.

———

Catty-corner to the block I grew up on sat an abandoned railroad freight yard. When I was in my early twenties my sister and I bought a dog, Wendy, and I would walk her through the lot at dusk. From the corner I could see the red neon lights of the PSFS building downtown, seven miles to the south. To the west, out beyond the lot's chest-high grasses grown up through cracked concrete, beyond the rise at the back rim of the yard that held the tracks, a tick to the left of the setting sun, blinked the red lights of Roxborough's giant radio towers, ten miles west of Frankford. Littered as it was with broken Rolling Rock bottles, the lot still conjured in me some kind of atavistic yearning: wilderness had reclaimed what had been a paved white sheet of city block.

The old factories in the neighborhood hugged the tracks; the second floors of these buildings all had big doors to load and unload the train. The factories were empty. Trains no longer ran through here. But they had run right behind the backyards of the houses on Sellers Street, at the south end of the lot, where my mother's mother grew up. On Orthodox, at the north end of the lot, where my mother's father grew up, you could stand in your front yard and hear the El going by four blocks away. Factories and trains had made the neighborhood—why else would all these thousands of people be living together in a few square miles of brick boxes?—and they had gone. So what made the neighborhood now?

In the late nineties a tall chain-link fence was erected around the freight lot. A few months later construction began and the whole block became a parking lot with a Jehovah's Witness Kingdom Hall set down in the middle. No more views of distant flashing lights. New brick buildings closing in. No open spaces abided. A place for worship would seem a net gain for the neighborhood, especially when it replaced an empty lot. There was something about the sustained emptiness of that space, though, that had felt like an honest expression of the neighborhood's present.

———

After the newspaper king removal, Janie agrees to go out with me. We discover in my parked car that all the hours of talking we'd done the summer before are now channeled into a crazy genital-liquefying attraction. I'd never felt anything like it. It only takes a few nights of dropping her off at 3:00 a.m. at her parents' house before her mother tells Janie we'll be murdered parking like that, and if we want to "spend time together," we should do it in their basement.

Maybe because I'm so short on experience being with a pretty girl with soft lips and dreamy eyes, especially one who reads good books and seems to like me, I fall into an immediate daze. I am in love in those early weeks with what Janie gives me, which, I see now but only felt then, is a way out of myself. I tell her after a night of making out in the basement, after only a few weeks of dating, that I love her. We haven't slept together yet. We haven't even talked much in these weeks since we spend all our time together chewing each other. I startle her when I say it and she doesn't say a word in response. Part of me knows when we hang out that she's somehow reserved, hiding something, that even though she can talk a mile a minute about her sisters or the movie we've

just seen, in our most intimate moments she radiates what I
recognize from myself and my mother and sister as a deep,
taciturn sadness. That suggested in her purposefully unmet
looks is the presence of a wall that may be holding back an
ocean. But I am a baby at love, powered only by blind need,
and so I ignore any signs for caution, keep pursuing, pushing,
flirting, hoping to have it said back. I say it because I want
something, just as my dad had when he said it to Theresa and
me. I need to hear it back more than anything else in life. I
wouldn't have blurted it so early otherwise, but of course I
can't see that. As the summer goes on I understand that I do
love Janie, and it's a relief that I haven't been misled by my
needs, that I'd just needed to catch up to them.

———

A busy livery man collects grubby little handwritten checks
from funeral directors for twenty and thirty-five dollars.
On a good day you'd get two or three in the course of a few
hours, and since my dad was looking to this work more for
his bridge tolls and grocery money than for anything else, he
frequented a check-cashing place at Bridge and Pratt, which
is Northeast Philadelphia's public transportation hub, the
place where buses and trolleys meet the El's northern end
of the line. Until I was five my mother's parents lived a few
blocks from Bridge and Pratt, and I have memories of sitting
in the car at sundown with my dad on an evening in the late
seventies waiting for my mother to get off the El there so we
could go to her parents' for dinner. In those days, there was

an indoor skateboard park at Bridge and Pratt and a grocery store called Farmer's Choice. There was a diner there, too, the Continental, that my grandparents frequented. I remember being in it one night in 1979, with my mother and her brothers and sisters and their spouses, everyone meeting there to wait while my grandmother had surgery a block away in Frankford Hospital. Safe at night on the Avenue amid the cold, red cheeks of well-dressed, good-looking young professionals who loved me. My people. Bridge and Pratt in the late seventies was, I guess, like a lot of urban transit hubs: crowded, policed, dangerous if you were alone at the wrong time of night, but for the most part safe. By the late nineties it probably wasn't too different, but like so much of life in Frankford, it felt coarser, more stripped of anything that felt generous or bountiful of spirit. The check-cashing place was run by a guy named Glen, a decent-seeming man with a ridge of crude hair plugs running across the peak of his forehead. Glen knew Dad's name and said hello when we walked in. I liked this. I imagined maybe this was what life in the neighborhood was like for my grandparents at my age or even my parents: shopkeepers owning their places for years and decades, knowing you and your habits, what you wanted, whereas most of the neighborhood stores I frequented were chains—Acme, Rite Aid, Kmart—with huge staffs and heavy employee turnover and no owner, of course, maybe within a thousand miles. The only difference between Glen and those shopkeepers I would conjure from my grandparents' era was the half inch of Plexiglas between him and us, and the sawed-off shotgun that hung from two brackets in the glass at the level of his chest. "Have a good day, Will," he said. Dad said, "You too, Glen."

The next time we hang out, Janie tells me that in the past semester, just a few months before, the drama teacher she'd called her mentor, the one who kept telling this skinny girl how she'd have to lose weight to get any acting jobs, had put his hand up her skirt when they were alone in a classroom and tried to scare her into sleeping with him. A process began, she says, of her telling another teacher, then having to file a report, steps ultimately leading to the firing of this man for sexual harassment. I feel like I might fall over sideways. She has said the secret words out loud. She tells me this is why she's having trouble eating, why I only ever see her sucking breath mints and chewing gum, why she's always up for going out to the movies but never to a restaurant. When she tells her story I imagine my father as her violator. I am certain she'll end it with me if I tell her about him.

Janie loves me, too. She tells me so one night. And I love her more when I tell her, after weeks of avoiding it, what the charge had been against my father when he was fired. (The actual events were something I didn't know at this time. I'd never asked. I didn't want the extra trauma of hearing something worse than the gentle flirtation I'd hoped for.) She tells me she doesn't care. I can tell there's a feeling about the both of us, that we're helping the other come back to life after much sadness. We get comfortable in our routine that first summer—going out to movies, sometimes to bars that won't card her. One Monday night that August we watch from barstools as the president says, "I did have a relationship with Miss Lewinsky that was not appropriate." That's your problem, Bill. I've finally got a good thing going for myself.

Even though we're all turning twenty-three this year, Wilbur and Gazz are already with the women they'll be with until they die. Wilbur's been with Stefanie since we were fourteen. Gazz has been with Kelly since we were seventeen, and they have a three-year-old together. It's only natural I suppose that I start to think of Janie this way. My two best friends are locked up already, why shouldn't I be? It would be hard to do better than Janie. And why would I want anything different?

This is the way we knew: you settle where you grew up, with someone you grew up with. My aunts and uncles were married to people they'd known from high school or the years just after. Every aunt and uncle I have—my parents are each one of five—met their spouse within fifteen miles of William Penn's hat. When my parents were in high school, my dad's older brother was engaged to my mom's older sister. There were small inklings in me that I should leave Philadelphia, but nothing articulated. I assumed I would learn how to be an adult from proximity to the adults I knew. We were taught to be provincial, to trust the institutions and the places we came up in—school, parish, neighborhood. This was ingrained, the kind of life you left at your own peril. My parents had left it for two years in Gainesville and come right back. They had proved there's no use leaving.

———

One night the week before Thanksgiving 1998. Janie and I have been together six months. She's at her dorm, I'm home instant-messaging with Wilbur, and then we're joined by May, a friend of Wilbur's girlfriend, Stefanie, in the days when AOL let chatters go into a "private room." The three of us are only logged on for a few minutes before Wilbur signs off to go to bed. May and I have only met once, a few months before at a block party on Wilbur's street. I was attracted to her then, but I'd only been in her company for half an hour, with dozens of other people around. We had never talked privately at all. I knew nothing about her. Once Wilbur logs off, my mouth starts to water. It feels as if some entity outside my body is taking control of me. If I were a shark, my eyes would have rolled back in my head. And yet I have the feeling of seeing exactly what's going to happen. It takes less than five minutes for May and me to tell each other we're attracted. I ask her if she thinks I have the guts to come over to her house right then. It's one in the morning. She says no, she doesn't think I do. We go back and forth like this. I'm so fucking hard.

It's 1:30 when I leave the house, careful not to wake my parents. It's just like a removal. I have a street name and number on a sticky note on the seat next to me. When I get to her block I figure out which side's houses are even numbers. It's dark; I creep the car down the block until I see her sitting on the front step working a cigarette. I park. She says, "I didn't think you would come." I follow her into the basement. Her mouth tastes like smoke. Her breasts are heavy, bigger than my hands. We never undress. Just do it on her basement floor with *The People's Court* on the television. I'm driving home five minutes later.

The thing I tried not to think about was my father. I'd hated him for eight years for running around on my mother, and now I'd followed the first impulse, taken the first chance I'd had to cheat on someone I loved. What I had no idea about, what I was just getting my first hands-on lesson in, was making trouble. This is what you do when you're putting something off, avoiding. This is what you make: trouble. This is what keeps you safe from any real engagement with the girl you love, because now everything seems watered down, at a remove, not as serious as before, because now you have a secret and it takes the pressure off you having to meet expectations. Now you know for certain you can be secure in your misery. Now you know for sure this thing with Janie will never be truly good. You're safe.

Then a phone call came from a guy named Dave at a place called Brotherly Love Cremation. He was looking for a full-time driver, and Jimmy Dominic, a dispatcher at the livery company, had recommended me. It was as if the universe was asking itself, How can this idiot's life, blindfolded trudge that it's turning out to be, be made less shitty, yet more entrenched?

―――――――

When I was scuffling in these years I took solace in my sister's path. She had been the captain of the cheerleading team in high school. She was enrolled at Penn and lived in a dorm there. She had no problem living away from home, no problem making friends. She seemed happy.

And then she started to falter in her coursework. She was having trouble with her concentration and mood. A semester later she was flunking out of Penn. And then she was moving home to her childhood bedroom. And a few weeks later she was hired as a file clerk at a law firm downtown—a friend from the neighborhood got her in—and going out to the bars every weekend with high school friends. I've wondered what screwed her up. Was she depressed by our parents, was it my example as the fuckup older brother that knocked her out of orbit? Or was it something else? Was there something about getting close to some tangible success that had spooked both of us? If we breezed through college, what would it have meant for our positions in the world we knew? How would success and happiness have estranged us from our parents?

―――――――

Death, death, death. All the roads led back.

A biology-class skeleton on its back in a pizza oven, this was my first impression of a corpse in flames.

"Not bad, right?" Dave said.

This burning corpse is somehow easy to take. One practicality helps: the door to the oven stays shut for at least the first half hour of the cremation. The closed door helps the temperature rise at a time when the only goal is igniting the body in a hot chamber. Also, we're never fully certain that the body and the casket are free of objects like a pacemaker or a beer can that could explode at high temperature and throw shrapnel. (Once every few weeks, in the first few minutes of a cremation, we'll hear what sounds like a bus's backfire and know we've missed a pacemaker.) This is all to say that by the time it's okay to open the door slightly to check on the cremation's progress, nothing reminiscent of life remains: no hair, no fleshy features to recognize, of course no writhing under the flames. (How can he just lie there?) Plus we're facing the crown of the skull, not a familiar or generous angle. All of these make it easier to translate what we're witnessing into a different kind of code than the language of everyday experience. If on this first night I'd seen skin melting off a face, if I'd seen breasts catching fire, toes crumbling off, if I'd seen the distinguishing features—his nose purple-veined from drink, her green eyes and fat ass—maybe I wouldn't have been able to do the job.

Brotherly Love Cremation was a garage in a place called the Frankford Arsenal, an old military weapons depot along the Delaware in Bridesburg, the next neighborhood east from Frankford. Inside the garage sat two cremation machines, with a gap between them wide enough to park a Ford Econoline van. Further back was a small office, the roof of which served as a loft for storing cardboard caskets. Electricity ran into the garage but not water, so there was a Porta Potti outside and a sink in the office with a foot-pumped spigot for hand washing.

I got there that first day at four o'clock dressed, as Dave had specified on the phone, in a polo shirt and jeans. He sent me out to a funeral home in Kennett Square, the so-called mushroom capital of the world, a fifty-mile one-way drive from Northeast Philly, the last stretch of it through the horse farms and cornfields of the Brandywine River Valley. The funeral home smelled of lilies. A pretty, middle-aged secretary offered me one of her baby carrots. She signed a slip I'd brought confirming my receipt of Mr. Smith's body, then led me to the walk-in refrigerator, where I met one of their funeral directors, a gray-haired, googly-eyed Marty Feldman look-alike named Clement. He and I rolled Mr. Smith, who lay there in his cardboard casket atop a four-wheeled cart called a church truck, out the back door of the funeral home to the back doors of the van. We positioned him so that the lighter end of his box, the foot end, would go in first. After a bit of small talk during which Clement lit a cigarette—"The Phillies?" he said. "You still like those assholes? I gave up after they went out on strike"—I was back on the road. It was like a removal but without the suit, without the odors, without touching flesh, and without exposure to a family's grief.

On the way back I sat in the holiday traffic of people headed to the Jersey Shore. I got back around 7:30. Dave was waiting for me. Once we pulled Mr. Smith's casket out of the van and logged in his paperwork, Dave said, "Come here. I want you to get used to this."

He walked over to a cremation machine and pressed the button that raised its door. "What do you think?" he said.

———

Fists were magnetically attracted to Gazz's face. A lot of the times we went to bars, after hours of talking quietly and drinking, a switch would flip near closing time and he would pick a fight. Somebody with no ill intentions would bump him on the way to the dance floor and Gazz would put a hand on the guy's shoulder and spin him around. "You startin' shit?" he would say. The guy might say, "I don't want any trouble," or sneer and say, "What you gonna do?" but either way Gazz would throw the first punch and then it was just a waiting game until the haymaker to his jaw arrived. He was slight but strong, the son of a linebacker, and ran five miles a day. It's just that he was always wasted. So he'd throw an off-target, listless punch and then often get creamed in the mug by some adrenaline-fueled dude who'd had two beers. And it wasn't like he started with the small guys in the bar. He had a knack for finding big guys who could really give him what he wanted. One night he started a fight in a place called Who's on Third? Not much happened before the bouncer, a hulking guy—maybe five ten, 250—dragged him outside. "Go home!" the bouncer said. He had Gazz by the front of his shirt and was leading him across the street away from the bar. When they crossed the street, Gazz got in his face and raised his fists. "Come on! Hit me, you bitch! Hit me!" The bouncer put his fists up but clearly didn't want to do anything. He had eighty pounds on Gazz. "Go home!" he said again. Gazz said, "Hit me, you pussy." He took a step toward the bouncer. "Hit me! Come on. I want a fair one." He took another threatening step toward the bouncer and cocked his fist. The bouncer snapped one left jab on Gazz's mouth that buckled his knees. The bouncer reached out and caught him so he wouldn't hurt himself on the fall. He stood over him and asked if he was all right. That's when I came over and hailed a cab.

I didn't fight. Ever. I didn't get excited. I picked Gazz up. I scolded him for fighting. You have a baby, I told him. But I didn't really mind. Not in my silent depths, below my schoolmarm pose. I let Gazz be the vicar of my violence, even though you could've powered a forklift with the stopped-up rage in me.

———

I drove around picking up befores and dropping off afters. My coworkers were Dave, the owner and manager of the business, and his friend from mortuary school, Omar, who did the cremating. Dave had been a champion pole-vaulter in high school. Omar had been an all-city quarterback. They were both trim and strong and in their mid-thirties. When they weren't talking about work details, their conversations didn't veer far from sports and TV and their wives and kids and their mutual friends from the old days. When a funeral director dropped off a body, often he or she would sit and chat and have a drink of water from the bubbler. Depending on how busy the day was sometimes a director would stay for an hour or longer. While Dave seemed to enjoy these little stop-and-chats generally, he could sometimes be distracted by phone calls or paperwork. Never, though, would you see a happier, more engaged, more jolly cowboy during these visits than Omar. He would guffaw at stale jokes loud enough that I could hear him out by the cremation machines, which whined like jet engines. And yet without fail, when the director left, Omar would frown, shake his head, and say something like "What a fucking dickhead." I immediately liked Omar. He reminded me of my grandmother, who pulled the same trick to the same effect, their comedy coming from a disgust at their own insincerity as much as with the objects of their scorn. "Don't ever grow up to be a funeral director, Andrew," Omar would say. The more miserable Omar got, the more Dave acted like nothing was wrong. It reminded me of my parents.

———

Dave wants to expand, to buy a third oven; the current place is barely wide enough for the two he has. There have been rumors, too, that the Arsenal will be sold to developers and turned into a Home Depot. So, in the winter of 2000, after several months of scouting new locations, Dave buys a building about two miles further north on State Road, a block west of the river. This is the balls of the city, the place where men spend the day, home to sex shops and strip clubs and truck-stop cheesesteak stands, all meant to lure workers from these industrially zoned blocks where landscapers house their machines, where big rigs are sold, where roofers store their tar and ladders, where auto-glass guys keep shop. These are the kinds of places a residential neighborhood doesn't want, but needs and keeps nearby, dark necessities like the basements of hospitals, like a crematory. The new place opens at the end of March.

I'd been riding my bike two miles each way to the Arsenal. Citizens enjoy throwing half-full beer cans out their pickup truck windows at me. The gentler types yell "Faggot!" or try to hit me with lungers. Gangly, rosy-cheeked, with short black hair and a pair of Henry Kissinger's castoff frames worn without irony, I pedal my bicycle through these joyless and increasingly murderous river wards. It's as if I'm the star of *Pee-Wee's Big Cremation Adventure*. A growing part of me has settled into bemusement by how little I belong around here.

One day I'm in my neighborhood's Wawa convenience store, across from the Kmart and Acme. I spot Lucas, a boyhood friend I haven't seen in several years. He's grown up to be just as relatively short as he was as a kid. He's deeply tan with eyes almost clear blue. He tells me he's tending bar at a place under the El, near Northeast Catholic, and that he's been teaching himself to throw knives. A fellow autodidact, I tell him I'm teaching myself to cremate. He tells me also that he fixes up old cars to sell.

A few days after I see him in the Wawa, Lucas and I are out on Roosevelt Boulevard in an old white Saab 900 hatchback I've agreed to buy from him, the one slight problem being that I can't drive stick. So this day we're jerking and lurching in midday traffic and he's next to me, neither nervous nor impatient. "You're fine," he says. I feel powerless to tell him how much I liked him as a kid. I want to tell him how much he reminds me of the last days of my childhood before the house went silent, how he was the only friend who came and spent a day with me when I'd broken my leg. I don't say any of it. We just talk about the car and how his little sister, who's friends with mine, is doing. He seems different than I remember him, like maybe he can still laugh but has a further distance to travel to get there. I wonder to myself about the cause of the distance and guess he senses some of the same in me. Maybe it's just because we're not familiar anymore. Maybe another day or two of hanging out would cure it. I come by a day later with the thirteen hundred dollars we'd agreed on. I'd asked the bank clerk for all of it in twenties because I thought it would help him, they'd be easier for him to use than hundreds. When I hand him the extra-large wad he exhales out between his lips—such an amateur—and doesn't look at me. He sighs again in the course of rubbing free each of the sixty-five bills. We never speak again.

————

June 2000. I have a car, a girlfriend, I've been making a good salary at the crematory for a whole year. Moving to my own apartment seems likely soon. I'm feeling like maybe this is what a normal twenty-four-year-old feels like. Things with my dad are better than in a long time. We'd spent a year and a half working the same job, and that seemed to let a little air into our relationship. If I'd just met him on the job, he would've been my favorite guy to work with. He always volunteered to take the heavier end, which most guys didn't do when they worked with a kid. He was versatile and generous in conversation. He could talk about sports or movies or the news. He let other people talk. It was nice to be with him as a likable acquaintance, not the guy who had crushed my mother.

In mid-June, Mom and her siblings throw a big party at a Knights of Columbus hall for their parents' sixtieth wedding anniversary. I bring Janie as my date. Someone's hired a swing band made up of sickly-looking eightysomethings fronted by a porky old chanteuse in a Mae West wig. Good for me to be among the living elderly! A banquet of liver spots, walkers, cataract sunglasses, girdles. The marriage in my nose of liniment and floral perfumes and hot roast beef. I see couples in their eighties attempt a jitterbug. At work I see only people on the losing end of their eighties. I see hundreds of old women a year that for me become one Mildred. Mildred dies in bed with her wedding portrait hanging in sight. Mildred's been a widow for twenty-five years. Mildred's at peace now, her daughter tells us, reunited with her Jack. Mildred and Jack. And now I'm in a hall watching a dozen Mildreds and Jacks spin around the linoleum to "Moonlight Serenade." Mildred and Jack smiling at my parents, who have been asked to pose together for a photo. Mildred and Jack forever.

———————

The next morning is Father's Day. Theresa and I go downstairs to the kitchen together because we have gifts for Dad—cigars, a book about Ireland's horses. Mom's not home. Dad's sitting there waiting for us. His eyes are red.

"Where's Mom?" I say.

He says, "We need to talk." We haven't had a family talk since he told us he was fired. "Your mother and I, we haven't gotten along for a long time. We had a talk this morning." This makes two talks for him in one day, a Meredith record. "We decided it's best that I move out."

All the evidence of the last ten years has shown that our parents have stayed together only out of some arcane Catholic obligation, or maybe because they're each too broke to live alone and raise kids. All four of us have known that whenever the two of them can live separately our relief will be spectacular. So why is the news so upsetting? Theresa and Dad go into the same hug they'd made ten years before. I don't get up this time. I sit. What a fool I am for feeling shocked. There's a sense, I think, that we have spent many years and much psychic energy holding together what had once been a solid family. For them to split up may be the healthiest move, but it's also the moment when all four of us will have to accept our failure. Mom and Dad admit their twenty-eight years of marriage will end. Theresa and I admit the folly of our hanging around the house into our twenties, acting as fingers in the dike, wallowing in depression and weird jobs, and now we'll finally have to face life outside the shelter and privacy of our parents' home.

I call Janie at her job as a hostess at a restaurant, and I call Gazz. The three of us meet in Society Hill at the end of Janie's shift and walk around downtown. They just let me talk. I feel beaten up, weak and tight and sore and nauseous.

I go back to the house later in the afternoon. Mom still isn't there. When she gets in she starts crying. She hugs me and says, "We stayed together for you."

Years later my mother will tell me that the day before that Father's Day in 2000 when Dad told us he was leaving, just a few minutes before we left the house for my grandparents' anniversary party, she answered a call on our kitchen phone from a stranger who didn't identify himself. He asked for Mrs. Meredith.

This is she, Mom said.

I'm calling to tell you your husband is sleeping with my wife.

––––––––––

I spent most of the summer between my freshman and sophomore years of high school indoors wearing a leg cast that came up nearly to my crotch. Lucas was one of the only friends who came over to visit, the only one who stayed for hours. One afternoon the two of us sat in the living room screening the John Candy vehicle *Uncle Buck*. He signed my cast. He had been the goalie the last few years I played soccer, and his mom and my dad had gone to grade school together. I thought he was the funniest kid on the team.

Just a few weeks before I broke the leg, six months before my dad was fired, Lucas and our friend Joey and I were playing basketball in our regular spot, a driveway behind a row of houses on Overington Street. Maybe a hundred yards away, traffic went by on Large Street, which ran perpendicular to the driveway. That block of Large had no homes on it, just an empty factory, a retired train trestle, the field where we played soccer, and an empty gravel lot. Cars flew along this stretch because there were rarely any parked cars and not many people on foot except during soccer games.

That day, while we played ball, we heard a car racing down Large. We saw it come up from behind and then cut off a car traveling at a normal speed, so that both came to violent stops. The driver of the attacking car got out. He was maybe eighteen. He started yelling, "Why'd you cut me off? Get the fuck out of the car!" The other driver was forty-five or fifty, heavy, bald. He got out. I don't know why. Maybe he thought he could calm the kid. Maybe he had a son that age at home. "Come on, I didn't cut you off," he said.

"You cut me off."

"We both had a stop sign."

"You fucking cut me off!"

The older guy tried to get back in his car. The kid surprised him, grabbed the front of his jacket and spun him down to the curb. The kid hustled to his car and opened the passenger door, pulled out a crowbar. As the kid approached, the older guy raised his open hands and said, "Please." The kid—I remember long, dirty blond hair and a white baseball cap worn backward—

slammed the bar across the man's upper arm. The kid pivoted and brought the bar back down across the other arm. The man fell and slumped to his side; he couldn't completely manage curling into a ball, and the kid unloaded strike after strike. As the kid tired out, the gaps between hits got longer and the guy was crying, "No. Please." I don't know what made the kid stop. Maybe his arms were too tired, maybe a car driving by on Arrott, out of our sight, spooked him. But after about twenty blows he trotted back to his car and peeled away.

A neighbor on the block, the guy who let us play at his hoop, a man whose name I forget but whose hawk nose and modest mullet perfectly suggested the golfer Greg Norman, was standing with us now. He had heard the yelling and come out his back door. He walked down the driveway to the victim. This is how the memory ends, with Greg Norman approaching this middle-aged man who's crying on his back on the curb of that barren block, trying with broken arms to clutch himself, while I'm standing a hundred yards away with my friends, cradling a basketball. In this way, as much as through the good times, I have always been tied to Lucas. We'd witnessed something awful together, one failure of civilization that must have burrowed as deeply into his psyche as into mine, one incident that as much as any other signaled the dying of our neighborhood.

———

I don't know how it would have gone with Janie if things with my parents had been different. That summer of 2000 she asked me if I would think about moving to Brooklyn with her while she did grad school. I thought about it, but I couldn't see how I'd get a job that paid as well as the crematory. This was what I told myself and her. The truth, of course, was bigger. I didn't want to make that commitment at that age. I was as old as my father had been when he got married, and Janie the same as my mother, and for everyone else I knew, moving in with someone in your early twenties meant a lifetime hitch. And because I was scared of leaving Philadelphia.

Janie moved to New York in August, and I visited a few times. At the end of September she dumped me. I found out later that in that first month of school she'd started seeing a guy in her class. It seems obvious now. Of all the people I've known who've moved away for graduate school, I can't think of any who stayed with the boyfriend or girlfriend back home. But I hadn't met any of them yet then. And I couldn't see that really I'd been the one to break us up, that we'd been done from the day I told her I was staying put.

———

My normal day at the crematory looked like this: I'd get in at 11:00 and hit the road. I'd drive to pick up two or three bodies in the first hour and bring them back so Omar would have them there to burn. Then I'd go deliver the cremated remains that were due back and pick up the rest of the day's dead. While I was out I'd often get a call from Omar or Dave saying there was a new call on, could I swing by this or that funeral home and do the pickup on my way back? I was just like any other deliveryman, except I carried human cargo.

My favorite drives were out in Chester County, past horse farms with split-rail fences. I always thought of Mickey Rourke in *Diner*, a city kid driving through horse country, pulling over to chat up a beautiful blond equestrian. I never saw any stunners on horseback, but the rolling hills, trees, grass—the overwhelming windows-down bliss of it—would do something to me. It was like the beginning of *Moby-Dick*, the part about how all men crave being near water and can't explain why. Often those green drives would be the best part of my week.

Without a cassette deck in the van, most of the day I'd listen to sports talk or a station that played soft rock, my nostalgia growing every year for the radio hits of the childhood breakfast table, songs like "Sister Golden Hair" and "Doctor My Eyes."

———

And then somehow you find yourself naked in a Victorian house in the suburbs meatus to meatus with a manicurist you met in a bar while her parents—who don't much speak to each other; your initial conversational spark—attempt to soothe themselves to sleep in the next room with a machine that makes ocean sounds. The manicurist is ample, flirty, smart. She's made a studio of her parents' attic, where she uses the techniques of realism to paint movie aliens and human-size gerbils. Her little overbite, the smell of her neck like the sweetest taste of pork chop and apple sauce, the shine of her black bob—it feels like Godard or Yahweh Himself cast her in your life. Her ass in jeans alone takes months off your expected date of death. And all of it adds up to such a void of feelings for her that you suspect something's wrong.

And on the nights you don't see the manicurist you're dating a kindergarten teacher, but every time she gets undressed, maybe it's because she's blond, you see Janie's head on her body and you excuse yourself to the bathroom and splash cold water on your face.

And then you're out with the manicurist again at a bar downtown and on the way out of the place you see Lucas. You haven't seen him since you bought the Saab a year ago. He rolls through the intersection in an old gray, tinted-out Pontiac with his window rolled all the way down. His eyes are dark, heavy, dull. You focus on each other, but neither of you raises a hand or even nods. A dark omen, you think, this pair of boys becoming men incapable of the most meager goodwill.

Another night the manicurist's sister and six-year-old niece do homework at their kitchen table and the manicurist pushes you down on the couch in the living room, maybe ten feet from the mother and daughter and just out of sight around the corner. You lie there still, wide-eyed at her bravado. She puts you inside her and loses herself in the ride, head back, eyes closed. She is both rider and bull. You're the ground, boy.

Wilbur and Gazz pick me up at the crematory for a Sixers game. I just have to reposition a body before I leave, make sure there are no parts left outside the range of the cremation burner's direct flame. They've never been here before. I ask if they want to watch.

"Dude. Yes," Wilbur says.

Gazz isn't interested. He stays off to the side.

Wilbur crouches like a catcher to see into the four-inch gap made by raising the door. With the long hoe I crumble the skull, giving the flame access to the brain. To position the leg bones under the burner, I extend the hoe out and slide it back along the oven floor like a croupier stick. As we're walking out to the car, Wilbur, in the same tone he'd have used to alert me to a pile of dog shit still fifteen feet in front of us, says, "There's no way this job won't mess you up down the road."

———

For years I've called that period of eleven years when my parents lived together without talking "the silence." They talked, though. They navigated the topics of acquaintances sharing a house: repairs, bills, can you pick me up at the mechanic's, pass the butter. But joy had gone. Dad could laugh when Mom was around, but his laughter made her quiet. Mom would laugh sometimes, but not when Dad was home.

Part of what they gave us in these years was a sense of careening, of drift, the notion that things aren't going well but change isn't within our power. I stayed in the funeral business almost exactly as long as they stayed together without sharing a laugh.

———

Summer of 2001 I went and visited Janie at her parents' house, a few blocks from Oakland Street. She was home from New

York for a few days. I walked over building myself up, hoping that when she saw me, when we talked, she'd want to get back together on the spot. I remember such a response in my body—cold and twitchy—the closer I got to her house. When I got there she was in the living room. I'd forgotten how beautiful she was. Lips, teeth, eyes, skin, hair—all her goldenness both standing for itself and suggesting all beauty, all of it seeming to vibrate like a Terrence Malick wheat field at sunset with the insects miked. I hated my brain for registering her allure more now than at any time in the last year we were together. Her sisters were there, too, and her mom and her sister's baby. We made small talk. She never suggested that we should go somewhere private. We just stayed in the living room as two members of the larger group. I was the visitor. I left after half an hour. When I did, she gave me the kind of hug you give an old aunt. She thanked me for coming. You only thank people for coming, I realized that day, when you want them to leave.

———————

That summer my parents finally split up. My mom moved across the river to New Jersey to be closer to her elderly parents. My dad moved around the corner to Orthodox Street. His house had belonged to a couple for the whole length of their marriage, and Dad bought it from the old widow. A corded telephone was mounted on the kitchen wall with a brass plate adhered to the length of the receiver engraved with the name of the late homeowner, WALTER REUSS. The kitchen stove had lasted from the fifties, a gas model whose every use required a match. The whole back half of the house was sinking, so that the windows and doors didn't close flush but let in triangles of light and draft.

———————

The two years with Janie had helped my confidence. I could approach anyone with a few drinks in me. And over email, with no courage required and room for endless charm, I was unstoppable. I was driving my old Saab around, cranking Pavement, making decent money. Living in my movie. Racing my problems. Trying to drink more dance more go to the movies more fuck more speed everything up so that I wouldn't have to be alone. And there began to happen "the scene at the curb."

I would start every relationship after Janie, even the ones with absolutely no promise, with grand romantic questions. What will it be like when she meets my family? How will she look in her wedding dress? I would woo her, we'd date for a few weeks or a few months, and then would begin the process of being slowly disappointed. God, do her feet really look like that? Her waking-up face is not okay. Did she really just say that Superchunk, the least talented, least inventive band writing songs in English, is better than Pavement? Her mom's obese. So when it came time to get invited along on a family vacation, or did I want to meet her best friend and the best friend's husband, or if a party was coming up that I didn't want to take her to because I thought there would be women to meet, I'd flake. Stop calling. Sometimes I had the courage or the stupidity to say something in person. But inevitably it would end with her tracking me down on the phone or knocking on my door and I'd step outside and inevitably she would wind up crying at the curb next to her car and I would be stone-faced and then we would always be delivered to the same moment. She would ask, "Don't you feel anything?" And I would stay unmoved, with my eyes cast down, and she would cry harder for a bit. I wouldn't say a word, but a ridiculous thought would form: I'm jealous of your crying. And then at some point her face would stiffen into a determined frown. I'm not letting this asshole see one more tear. She'd gather herself and drive away without looking at me, and I'd think maybe she'd been infected. Maybe my failures, my cowardice, whatever damage had been done in my parents' house, had created a disease in me, an infectious coldness, and I was passing it on to one young woman after another. The irony being that the boy with the ice disease spent his days lighting fires.

How much pain lodges in the body? How much love? How much knowledge? How many resources unquantifiable do we blow away at nineteen hundred degrees? What does it mean to reduce a woman to five pounds of powdered bone in one three-hundred-thousandth the time she lived? I didn't think of these things at all during the years I worked with bodies. Never did I hold the dead in mind. Never could I bring myself to calculate the import of the work.

Here in my very hands, a naked woman. I'm touching her

chest, feeling for a pacemaker. I'm massaging soap onto her knuckle to jimmy loose her wedding ring. What have her fingers touched, I should wonder. How has my curiosity gone so numb? What have her eyes seen? The winds of which far-flung beaches have blown through this hair? Or have these toes only ever felt Jersey Shore sand? What kinds of people did this heart love? Were you a good girl? Just the hubby then? Or did you get around? What did your mother call you as a baby? Did you like a drink? What made you spiral? Any regrets? What kind of man was your father?

All the connections and possibilities and time in her body, all the links to all the time and bodies of everyone she had ever known and had touched, and from there links to everyone who had ever lived, back to the caves, back to the ooze. And as I'm closing the lid on her casket what I'm really thinking of is the Sixers game tonight and how I can't wait to see Wilbur and Gazz.

———————

Frankford had become unpleasant, lonely, less civilized, steadily more dangerous. The thought of Dad buying a house there in his middle fifties was an anxious one for my sister and me. One Sunday afternoon he called me in tears. Could I come over? I don't think he'd ever asked me so nakedly for help. He'd been out walking his dog, Wendy, a little beagle mix, when she was set on by a free-ranging, collarless pit bull. The thing had Wendy's whole head in its mouth, swinging her like a chew toy, before Dad was able to kick the attacker's ribs hard enough to break the frenzy. When I got there he was still red-eyed, shaky. After a while I understood that there wasn't anything I could do in a practical sense—the dog would see a veterinarian the next morning for the weepy puncture wounds dotting her face—but that Dad needed me there. He needed calm in the house. He seemed older to me that day. It felt easier to love him.

———

One night in a bar downtown I run into a guy named Tim Simone. I'd taken his computer science class my first year at La Salle, almost ten years before. Part of what he taught us was how to maintain our operating system. One day's lesson was how to "defrag." We watched as little primary-colored blocks fled across a white field, scattered groups of information reuniting in their original form, regaining the strength that comes, apparently, from being together in the place they belong. I'd liked Tim because he was young—maybe thirty— and showed no signs of knowing who I was. At the end of the semester he made me a mix tape heavy with Joe Jackson songs.

When I see him at the bar I tell him that the year I was in his class was only a few years removed from my father having been fired from La Salle. He asks my dad's name. He says, "That was your dad? Wow. I never heard the whole story of him and that woman."

I think, What woman? But I don't say anything. I shrug my shoulders. We wander over to the jukebox to look for "Steppin' Out."

We park, Gazz, Wilbur, and I, in the lot of a place called Jetro, a cash-and-carry food wholesaler next to Veterans Stadium, a block away from the building where we'll watch the Sixers play (in an arena whose name changes every few years after each new merger of the monolithic bank that owns the naming rights), and stand around the open trunk of the car killing as many beers as we can before the start of the game. Although we always miss the start of the game. We stand here forty-five minutes or an hour arguing Beatles vs. Stones or trying to remember the name of the kid in homeroom who shat himself during a fire drill. We talk about sports, our girlfriends, our neighborhoods, bands we like. In this circle we form, we claim what has been bestowed to us neighborhood boys, this legacy of drunkenness and spectator sports and the sun setting behind refineries. We claim each other: our reward for not leaving home, our reward for loyalty and cowardice. Just as my parents had been each other's reward. Wilbur usually turns up his car stereo to torture us with one of his favorites, something like Skid Row or Sepultura, and keeps the car doors open for more volume. After a few beers we start sneaking off one at a time to piss next to the shielding height of the nearest SUV. Sometimes we throw a football. Sometimes we heckle fans from other teams. The spell breaks when we realize we're the last ones in the lot. It's after seven. Time to chug and jam cans down our pants.

On the night in May 2001 when the Sixers beat Milwaukee to go to the NBA Finals, we were so drunk after the game that Wilbur—who had, almost so inexplicably that it seemed normal, found a box of fluorescent tube lights in the parking lot—wound up in the middle of Tenth Street throwing one bulb at a time high in the air, so that when each one hit the blacktop it popped like fireworks, leaving a white cloud at his feet. Cars drove by honking, fans yelping, high-fiving him, waving Sixers towels. At some point he took off his shirt and threw it to the curb. He lofted more bulbs. More fireworks. More high fives. More honking. How could there possibly be no cops around? There weren't. He dropped his shorts. He was skipping around with his shorts at his ankles screaming, "Sixerrrrrrs!" He was wearing only white underpants and sneakers. Excessive honking and hollering from all parties. He dropped to the ground on the yellow dividing line in the middle of Tenth Street and did push-ups over the broken glass. Then he drove us home.

On the present night, more sedate by half, Wilbur says to us on the way out of the arena, "What? Do you want to go to Slippery When Wet?"

A tiny place with low ceilings that could just as easily have been an AMVETS hall, Slippery When Wet was in no sense meant for gentlemen. The employees tended to be tattooed with garish implant scars. A few years after this night the place was raided by the FBI, and its co-owners—graduates of our fair alma mater, Northeast Catholic—were arrested on gun charges. (I think the FBI was disappointed because their investigation—like so many in Philadelphia—reportedly involved public corruption, not guns.)

Gazz had never been inside a strip club before. I'd been maybe ten times, a few for bachelor parties, and Wilbur and I had gone just the two of us a few times. Speaking at least for the clubs in Northeast Philadelphia, we went to these places less for eroticism and more for the reasons one would watch a sword swallower. Wilbur was always best in these situations. Unlike Gazz and me, he wasn't shy with strangers. He made small talk that night with even the most vacant dancers, of which there was no shortage. He was engaged in this when, I don't know why, I started rocking back and forth in my chair, staring at the floor. I heard Wilbur tell a woman, "He's retarded." And then I heard Gazz say, "He's our brother. We're just getting him out of the house for a night." "Aww," I heard her say. Then she was on my lap. I was twenty-seven and big—six two, 210 pounds. I was channeling Lennie from *Of Mice and Men.*

"Y'avin a good time, hon?" she said. I nodded yes. And that was that. Probably every woman working that night spent time on my lap. I didn't pay a dime. A parade of flesh, a comedy of arms legs breasts asscheeks summoning no feelings about sex, just as the festival of death at work every day stirred no feelings about life.

My life had become bodies all day long and a body at night. I was living the inverse of a Buddhist inversion—if I concentrated hard enough, the ancient, rotting woman in my hands at work would at night become a beautiful naked girl in my bed, or on my lap. I barely felt a thing about any of it except wanting to feel more.

One day in the office Dave asked me about the latest woman I'd been dating. She worked with kids and ran marathons. I told him it had ended badly, as usual.

"She sounded great for you!" he said. "What was the problem?"

"I just, you know, I didn't feel it."

He looked at me, but I could tell he was holding back what he wanted to say. I loved Dave. For me, depending on the circumstance, he was a boss, an older brother, and a father. Because he was so fastidious, he could be hard to work for sometimes, but I always felt we deeply respected and liked each other. Finally he said, "You need to let yourself be loved, Andrew."

I let out a laugh. Which of his wife's magazines had he gotten this from? You read this on the toilet, right? But even so, he'd been with his wife for twenty years. They had three kids. He knew that exchanging love and trust was the real entry to adulthood, and here I was still fucking around, holding myself back from serious engagement in love or career for reasons more mysterious to me than they should have been. Let yourself be loved—I went home that night and wrote it down on the back of a coffee receipt and slipped it in my wallet.

And yet.

Still I skulked onto the darkened doorsteps of the apartments of young women who'd promised to open their doors. Crept out of the shadows long enough to be taken in and then up to their bedrooms, and though not blessed with a forked penis I was as quiet as a possum and as businesslike, and as blind as the possum is, I was blind to what all this skulking around meant. I was dumb when it came to sensing that these women wanted to settle down and wanted to love someone and found my sweetness and mildness irresistible even though those traits were merely vestiges of my childhood rather than reflections of genuine character. I'd learned merely to use them to deflect attention. Oh, what a sweet boy he is. What a sweet boy. This is how many of these young ladies thought of me right up until the first day I didn't answer their phone calls or was spotted with another young lady walking hand in hand just a block away. What a slinking, creeping possum of a low-down carrion eater. Of course this is why the possum scares me. The possum is a coward. He avoids conflict by disengaging, by hiding behind his open eyes. Some think he's cute, some think he's vile. But regardless of how he handles himself, the possum does his job. He cleans up the dead. He eats carrion so we don't have to smell it, see it, catch its disease. He's evolved to dispose of our trash. I, too, made a life of disposing of carrion. Put you in your box and roll you into hell. I was terrified of the possum, for in that filthy trash-can sitter I saw myself.

———

Janie called me one day, long after the hairdresser and the kindergarten teacher, a few years deep into the scenes at the curb.

"I think about you," she said.

This is the part in the movie when the ex he's been consumed with finally wants him back. This is the point where after all that obsession, with the chance to have her back, he walks away, realizing the fever's broken, forgiving her, but having safely reached a place where she can no longer hurt him. Or, after much tribulation, he loves her anew, finding his salvation in their reunion. We started sleeping together again, and after a few weeks of menacing her with my old grievances, I dumped her like I had all the other women I dated. I didn't register even a pang. I was no longer paralyzed but truly dying. I had to get as far away from Philadelphia as I could.

5

Hummingbirds, jasmine, unknowable Range Roving gazelle women, empty sidewalks, sharp-peaked horizons. Los Angeles, I am here to live.

I left Philadelphia in May 2004 with no plan other than to sleep on my cousin Jeremiah's couch in Los Feliz and find any job I could. After a month of looking I hooked up with a temp agency. My first day I arrived prepared for "light construction" at a huge dirt expanse directly inland from the beach. From the looks of it I expected a job along the lines of shoveling a ditch or hauling trash out of a building meant for demolition. There were earthmovers and backhoes, a series of office trailers, and a tent as big as the roof on a good-size single home. The air rippled with the smell of my fellow workers' suntan lotion. This would do. A far cry from everything my working life had been.

I went into the trailer that fronted the street and told them I was from the temp agency. A woman led me to a little out-of-the-way corner of the operation. There sat a dusty, sun-bleached Shaker-style kitchen chair under a small white plastic tarp, and in front of the chair lay a dozen plastic buckets filled to the top with red earth. "What we need you to do," she said, "is to sift through these buckets looking for bones."

The plan for this land had been to build student housing for Loyola Marymount, but the diggers had unearthed a Native American village, and specifically a pit of bones where they suspected enemies killed in battle had been dumped. They were finding piles of bones, some with arrowheads still stuck between ribs. That's what I was to sift through, dirt from the burial pit. I guess someone at the temp agency had read my résumé.

Los Angeles, I am here to sift your buckets of death.

Because of provincial resentments, mostly sports-borne, I had never liked New York. Manhattan felt to me like an even less likable version of downtown Philadelphia, one infused with an even more naked anxiety, more and taller gray buildings, thicker, more frenzied mobs of people, the same weather, only without any of the friends that made my hometown palatable.

A few months before I went west, I had finally finished my college credits and graduated from Temple on my fourth try. I had started back the previous fall, still working part-time at the crematory, and something was different: I studied. I felt motivated. Maybe it was because I was ten years older than when I'd started college, but I motored along and finished two years of credits in one calendar year. I felt proud in a way I didn't expect. I couldn't explain it, but I felt like maybe some small progress was being made toward becoming someone I could respect. Still I finished without any further plans. I carried the notion that if I kept going, got my master's degree and started teaching, like my father, then of course I'd get married like he had, and have babies like he had, and then everything else he had done to his life I would do to mine. In other words, if I went to graduate school, I would make a family and ruin it. I walked around feeling like a time bomb. I was destined to hurt people. Wasn't yet convinced that wallowing was more fraught even than following my dad to the deepest reaches of fate's path. Wasn't attuned to the irony that in trying to steer free of his fate I had followed him to the lesser of his two careers, the one he did only for money, the one lacking the redeeming pleasures of books and similarly curious people, that by letting myself slide I was living a life no one who loved me would have ever chosen for me.

My assignment at the burial ground lasted a few weeks and then I was given a new one, as a room service waiter in a hotel in Beverly Hills. The working conditions couldn't have been more different. Indoors, air-conditioned, posh. My first official act was to run a ramekin of barbecue sauce to the room of Ashanti, the princess of hip-hop and R & B. In the first few weeks I delivered an ahi tuna niçoise salad to a barefoot Angelina Jolie. I bore witness to Susan Sarandon's predawn visage. Sacha Baron Cohen answered his door in only tighty whities. Another night

I took a long order over the phone from a Mr. Pattonback. "Yes, Mr. Pattonback," I said. "Of course, Mr. Pattonback." It startled me how quickly I'd adopted such mannered servility. A few minutes later, when I knocked on Mr. Pattonback's door, Mike Myers answered.

And yet.

And yet, I wore my own white oxford shirt, black pants, black shoes. I was given a salmon-colored vest and tie that I kept in a locker in the hotel basement. I was working overnight, paid to serve invisibly, pushing a cart past the hampers and exposed plumbing of the underbelly of a huge residence full of temporary guests, creeping silently down carpeted halls that looked no different from those of some of the top-shelf nursing homes I'd taken people from. Even when other people were picking the jobs for me, I couldn't escape death. Looking back, that seems appropriate. Death wasn't done with me.

My favorite thing to do at the hotel was go to the roof at 3:00 a.m., the one reliably slow hour of the night. There was a pool up there, and I liked to stand by it along the waist-high concrete wall at the roof's edge and take in Los Angeles in the dark, at peace. Look north to Sunset's high-rises, beyond them the twinkling hills, pan east along the ridge to where I was living, by Griffith Park. It was the most exciting feeling I knew. Even if it took sleep to silence them, I was still surrounded, for an hour at least, by my people.

The last few nights of my hotel assignment I trained my replacement, a kid named Cory who had just graduated from USC, and who had worked as a fine dining waiter and knew much more about the work than I did, meaning he could uncork wine bottles. On my last night I took a call from a guest listed in the registry as Mr. Alonzo. He asked if we had Rosé. I told him I'd check and call him back. I went to the hotel bar, found a bottle on the wine list, and called him back from the bar phone.

"Mr. Alonzo, this is Andrew. Yes, we have Rosé."

"How much?"

"It's sixty dollars for the bottle, sir."

"Sixty? No, I want Rosé Cristal."

"Oh. Okay. Let me check, sir. Yes. Here it is. Okay. It's five hundred dollars, sir."

"All right. Bring it up."

So Cory and I brought up a cart with the Cristal in an ice bucket and four champagne glasses. I knocked at the door, and Mr. Alonzo answered in a white terry hotel robe. Maybe thirty-five, trim, with a shaved head, he looked like a softer DMX. Fat Joe's "Lean Back," a big hit that summer, played loud on the room's stereo. I wheeled the cart into the bedroom, which was lit very dimly by the bathroom vanity. Sitting up in the bed, covered to her hips by the comforter, was a beautiful, fully developed, topless woman, dead-eyed, a young Pam Grier's zombie stand-in.

It was too dark in the bedroom to open the champagne, so I asked Cory if he would do the honors in the light of the bathroom. When he left I stood in the most professional service industry pose I could remember having seen on television—spine erect, chin tilted up slightly, arms behind my back, right hand gripping left wrist like some royal toadie. Maybe something about the rigidity of my posture spurred on Mr. Alonzo, because while Cory worked in the bathroom, Mr. Alonzo climbed onto the bed on all fours, let himself under the comforter, took a second to position himself, and began pumping his hips while his friend, now flat on her back beneath him, closed her eyes and moaned.

Since her eyes were shut and Mr. Alonzo was concentrating, I gave myself permission to certify the undulating marvel of the waves and ripplets of her flesh in motion. How does a man even meet a woman who looks like this? I haven't seen ten women this gorgeous in my life, and this one's willing to have sex in front of room service. There is no limit, I thought, to the parts of our reason that can be silenced. The cork popped. Then Cory was back among us, bottle in hand.

Mr. Alonzo righted himself. Cory filled two glasses, at which time Mr. Alonzo said to us, "You're drinking, too."

"Sir," I said. I shook my head. "I'm sorry. We're on duty. We're not allowed to have a drink."

"You're drinking with me."

"We really can't," I said. "We still have a few hours left."

"How 'bout this? You're not leaving till you drink."

I looked at Cory, who pursed his lips. He didn't care. He wasn't in charge. And why should I have cared? I'd never be back here.

"All right," I said.

So Cory filled the other two glasses. We stood with them for a second before Mr. Alonzo said, "Let me toast." He raised his glass above his head, cleared his throat dramatically. "My name is Maximus Decimus Meridius," he hollered over the music. A friend has since told me that a mark of great fiction is for the action to feel both shocking and inevitable. Mr. Alonzo delivering a speech from *Gladiator* seemed to fit both criteria, but this was nonfiction. I quick-looked sideways at Cory and raised my eyebrows.

"Commander of the Armies of the North," he continued, "General of the Felix Legions. Loyal servant to the true Emperor, Marcus Aurelius. Father to a murdered son, husband to a murdered wife. And I will have my vengeance! In this life or the next!" His glass hung there above his head while Fat Joe ordered, "Now lean back lean back lean back lean back." Finally he touched his glass to ours and then to his bedmate's. I couldn't resist clinking with her, too, and then downed a gulp of pink champagne worth two weeks' grocery budget.

"Another one," Mr. Alonzo said.

So Cory filled our glasses again. The woman leaned toward him and held out her glass. She neither spoke nor smiled. They were dead to intimacy and here I was their witness, their possum.

That was my last night at the hotel, a weeknight in late September 2004. No more temp assignments came my way. I went back to Philadelphia over Thanksgiving weekend, thinking I'd make some money filling in at the crematory.

6

I told myself I'd be back only for the holidays, work part-time at the crematory to save some money, and head west again in January. I think I worked one day at BLC that December on what was more like a visit I was lucky enough to get paid for, as I sat in the kitchen and stuffed T-shirts bearing the crematory's logo into plastic bags—that year's Christmas present to funeral director clients. Dave had no open shifts, but I think he also suspected that if he gave me a bunch of hours I'd take the money and leave town again. So I didn't. (Why didn't I sell Christmas trees, bar back, wait tables, do removals for the livery company?)

———

"Meanwhile." That's the word. The one all musterable power is applied to ignoring, avoiding, never hearing. It means all that has happened and is happening while you careen. While you have skirted decisions, assiduously avoided assiduity, this has happened: you've lost friends, watched others marry and have babies, your parents have aged, people you love have died, your neighborhood has collapsed. My father turned into sex. I turned into running away. No one can get me. No one can make me.

In January, Dave offered me a few hours of work when he needed extra help cremating the Philadelphia medical examiner's cases. Once or twice a year he would win a contract from the city to cremate the unclaimed bodies in their morgue. Usually this meant fifty to sixty people. Some had never been identified. Most had been, but were never claimed by family. Each came with paperwork that contained a story put together by one of the ME's investigators.

> 6/11/98, Jane Doe found wrapped in carpet floating under Girard Point Bridge. Identified via dental records 6/17/98. Repeated calls to sister's house unanswered. 6/28/98 Sister answers phone. Says she hasn't spoken to deceased in eight years since deceased began drug use. Sister says she can't afford funeral for deceased. Leaves body in care of Medical Examiner.

If in a regular week we cremated forty to fifty bodies, adding fifty or sixty to a week's schedule meant the machines went nonstop from 6:00 a.m. to 2:00 or sometimes 3:00 the next morning. This also meant the bodies had to be meted out strategically over the day. After twelve hours of nonstop burning, the brick walls of the cremation chamber would glow orange, and the cardboard roller that we normally placed by hand in the front of the chamber would have to be dropped from the end of a pole to protect our arms and faces from the heat. Sometimes the machines would be so hot the roller would ignite on its own before the casket was placed on it, before the burners were even turned on. We'd have to knock the flaming roller to the back of the machine with the hoe and wait, hoping another minute with the door open would cool the chamber enough to proceed.

We'd save the lightest bodies for latest in the night; the more body fat, the greater the risk of the temperature spiking out of control and leading to mayhem, like uncontrollable black exhaust smoke (a serious taboo for a business trying to fly under the neighborhood's radar—you do what in there?—we didn't even have a sign), the smell of burning meat, or worse, boiling rivulets of body fat leaking out the front door of the machine, dripping down into the processing pan and onto the floor, leaving a grotesque cleanup task and an aromatic cocktail of chalk dust, basement mold, and the burnt black drippings in a roast pan.

So Dave sent Larry and me to the medical examiner's office in West Philly, near Penn's campus. I'd been home from Los Angeles five weeks. Larry drove.

"So it was good out there?"

"Yeah. I loved it." I told everyone I loved it—I had—even though I didn't really understand why.

"Get laid out there?"

"Nah." I had zero sexual currency in LA. No money. I had one friend, Jeremiah, and he wasn't getting laid either. I had no status in any way that would attract a sexual partner. Crushed Sprite cans in the gutter were touched more lovingly that year than were my genitals. But it didn't bother me much, I think because I knew it wouldn't last. I'd either get a job there, make friends, and have entrée to women, or I'd go back to Philadelphia, where I didn't have trouble. It was a relief to be away from relationships.

We were there to pick up six bodies. This meant we took six empty cardboard caskets with us and filled them one at a time outside on the loading dock, the January winds burning our fingers but tamping down the stink. The first man brought out to us had been dead seven years. He had been a "decomp" to begin with and now, after more than half a decade in the freezer, had started to thaw after having been lined up in the hallway waiting for us. To show us the toe tag, the pathology tech unzipped the body bag enough to reveal a single, shriveled purple foot—the desiccated skin had contracted enough to split—the toe bones seeming to have grown through the skin like flowers first breaching their buds. In one motion Larry's big belly withdrew and his head nodded forward.

"You okay, Lar?" I said.

"Yeah. I'm fine." He let out a deep exhale, then turned and threw up on the concrete. Two months before, I had been in Los Angeles bidding good evening to Angelina Jolie in her hotel room, snapping mental photographs of her elegantly tanned bare feet.

A few weeks later Dave took me to lunch at a dark, smoky little bar in Bridesburg. Once we'd been at the table and had talked about the Eagles—they were a few days from their first Super Bowl in twenty-four years—he pulled a folded legal pad page from his jeans pocket. He'd worked out a salary, plus money from arrangements and removals, and a 401(k) and health care package. "What do you think?" he said. I knew I was one of his favorites. He trusted me to get work done, to be friendly to funeral directors and comforting to families of the deceased. And he knew I was broke and crashing at my dad's house. The salary was much higher than he'd ever given me, even before the extra I'd make from handling direct cremation arrangements with families, something that had always been his and Omar's exclusive territory, and they were both licensed funeral directors. (Legally I could do everything but sign the statement of goods and services.) Between the crematory and my jobs in Los Angeles, I'd made a little less than nine thousand dollars the year before. I probably couldn't count on much more if I went back. Dave was offering me sixty thousand before taxes in exchange for a one-year commitment.

I asked if I could think about it. If I took it, I was admitting I'd failed in Los Angeles. I was a proud little bitch. Uselessly so. But it felt like I was admitting I'd failed in the only chance I'd ever get to leave Philadelphia and the funeral business.

That Sunday I was at my mother's for dinner and told her

what Dave had offered. "Oh my God," she said. "Tell him to hire me."

I took the job the next day. I called Jeremiah and told him I wasn't coming back to Los Angeles. I think he was less surprised than I was. I kept finding myself startled at my own careening into circumstances.

My dad took me in. I was too broke for my own apartment. One night I came home from a bar and saw a woman's purse on the recliner. It was too tacky to belong to my clotheshound sister. When I got upstairs he came out in the hallway red-faced, hair messed up, in his rugby shirt and jeans and socks. "Uhh, I have company over." I was now twenty-nine years old, living in an old lady's house, cockblocking my dad.

———

A few months after Dad was fired we were at my mother's sister's for dinner. I was fifteen. Like the rest of us, I was sad and fragile and down. I left the kitchen after clearing my plate and noticed on the counter a women's magazine with Sherilyn Fenn from *Twin Peaks* on the cover. At the moment I stopped to admire, my aunt and uncle walked into the room. My uncle said to my aunt, "Looks like the apple doesn't fall far from the tree." This was not lighthearted ribbing.

I never told my dad that story, but a few years ago he told me about going, as a boy, to visit his father, a commuter train conductor, at work. My father, maybe nine years old, watched a pretty woman exit the train, and from behind him heard one of his father's coworkers say, "Looks like the apple doesn't fall far from the tree."

———————

When I came back to work, Dave offered to pay my way through mortuary school. Most of the local funeral directors had gone to a night program at a community college just outside Trenton, and that's where he would pay for me to go. It would take two years and then I'd have a trade for life. I said I'd think about it. And I did. I considered the practical benefits of having this training that might've meant the lifelong guarantee of a paycheck.

But I hadn't proven to myself I could calm the general restlessness that led me so often to movie theaters, to record stores, to the bedrooms of the women I met, a restlessness that none of those quests soothed. Also, I feared grad school for the same reason I feared commitment in a relationship: I feared being fixed in space and time. If I went to grad school, that meant I had to choose one thing to be. If I went to mortuary school, the same. If I had moved to Brooklyn with Janie, the same.

I had seen my parents so obviously change after they'd fixed their positions in a marriage. Dad had gotten into Irish music and culture and Mom hadn't. She had gotten deeper into the church and Dad hadn't. I *knew* I would grow apart from any woman I settled down with. What I didn't know, or what scared me too much to consider, was that the thing I feared—picking one thing to be—could be the thing that saved me.

149

———————

We've lifted the cardboard box onto a church truck and pushed it from the garage into an air-conditioned holding room. Omar pulls on his gloves. "What's for lunch?" he says. We're two weeks into a quest to find the best chicken-parm sandwich in our little part of the world.

I take the lid off the box. He taps the dead man's left pectoral. "Is this the day you do it, Andrew?" He means slice into the dead man's chest.

"I'm just an English major," I say.

One night not long before this I'd seen a mouse in the crematory's garage. Later I couldn't find my cell phone. I hadn't remembered, of course, but it had been in my hand during the fear spasm that caused me to high-step like a drum major back inside the office. Dave found it the next morning beneath one of the parked vans. Like I've said, I was not a likely candidate for the funeral business. And yet. The rank smells of shit and purged bile and rotting flesh that came with this job never got to me. I never had a nightmare about snapped bones broken through skin, jaws lost to gun blasts, maggots crawling out of decomposing rib cages. I had a greater capacity for numbness than other people; the disengagement that settled on my house when I was a teenager had somehow inured me to the corporal miseries of the funeral business.

That said, I don't cut out pacemakers. It has less to do with revulsion than with wanting to avoid a deeper intimacy with the bodies. Scissoring into their flesh means a commitment, means I am of them. I would have no reason left not to acquiesce to Dave wanting me to go to mortuary school. Not cutting the flesh means I can maintain the notion of myself as a ham-and-egger just passing through, even though I've been here six years now. Nearly every time in the six years when either Omar or Dave has asked if I wanted to cut out the pacemaker I've heard myself say, "I'm just an English major." I still see myself after all this time as temporary help. Passing through, waiting for my life to begin, a glacial dilettante. This is not my career. No. I have one foot out the door, don't you see?

"Scissors?" he says. I hand people sharp things. I'm the funeral business equivalent of Hot Lips Houlihan.

"Where's Larry?" I say. Larry drives around to funeral homes all day in a champagne-colored Chevy panel van picking up bodies to be cremated and dropping off cremated remains. This is the job I did my first five years here. Since Los Angeles I've moved inside and started doing the bulk of the cremations. Omar is the office manager now. Dave has moved to a private office way up at the front of the building, on the other side of the cremation machines and the memorial chapel. In his office he maps out the long-term future of the business and, we suspect, takes naps and reads about fishing boats online and maybe masturbates to his wife's *People* magazines, which for some reason are delivered to the crematory. So it's Omar and I. And many days we'll call Larry at a quarter to noon to check his location, see if he's near a lunch place we like. We have a drawer in the office with at least fifty flyers from pizza places, sandwich shops, Chinese restaurants, bars hawking award-winning wings, sushi houses, barbecue pits.

Omar opens the shoulder snaps on the hospital gown to expose the chest and its bulge. He digs the sharp-pointed blade into the dead man's flesh. Omar weighs 230 pounds, lifts weights, and still you can see the strain in his forearms and wrists as he cuts.

"Have we tried Gearo's?" he says.

"Nope," I say. "Remember when we got spaghetti and meatballs from there on your birthday a few years ago?" Omar and I have had good times over the years.

He's cut a three-inch line revealing a red layer just below the skin's surface, beneath that a layer of knobby yellow fat, and then the pink muscle. He worms his fingers into the incision and retrieves the lump, a stainless-steel pacemaker the size of a change purse. He removes it slowly, and behind it two narrow metal coils that had run to the heart come free. I'm holding open a clear plastic bag, into which he drops the works. In a minute I'll put the bag into a casket vault in the garage with all the other metals that come out of our dead. "How much is left in petty cash, Andrew?"

"Fifty," I say.

He says, "You think we should get onion rings, too?"

———

When I was five years old, a boy we called Bugs lived next door with his grandmom Betty Lou. Before that and after, he lived with his dad in Jersey. He was a big-glasses boy, couldn't keep them on his nose they were so big. We'd have a tennis ball catch over the backyard fence. Once I got grass stains on my pale blue jeans. Sergio Valente. Mom said, "What did I tell you about these jeans? These are not play jeans." She rubbed a soapy paper towel on my knees while I stood there. One night Betty Lou lifted me over the waist-high chain-link fence between our yards. She and Bugs were roasting marshmallows. He handed me a stick flaming black at the end. When we were out of marshmallows we picked honeysuckle blossoms. Betty Lou showed us how to slice the flesh with a thumbnail, slide the stem out gentle, suck a bubble of juice.

Last year, I heard a story about Bugs. I hadn't seen him since 2001. He's living on Oakland Street still, but about a mile north of the block we'd lived on, in a house just off Cheltenham Avenue, a block from where my dad grew up. He has a new baby just home from the hospital. He's watching *SportsCenter* while mother and child sleep. He hears a man and woman arguing at the curb. He waits. The urgency in the voices heightens. Bugs—tall, muscled, gentle—lets himself out the door and down the steps. He says to the couple, "Hey, I don't mean any trouble. I have a baby sleeping inside. Can you move down the block?" The man turns and shoots Bugs in the chest. He dies there.

———

Part of coming back to the crematory means Dave wants me to make arrangements for cremation services. Most of the time this means sitting down in the crematory's kitchen—

our little break room has a refrigerator and a wooden table and chairs and we call it a kitchen—with a newly grieving family to pick out urns and prayer cards and collect all the information I'll need to write up a death notice. Every once in a while, though, there has been no death. Instead a person comes in to make what are called prearrangements, meaning a man or woman, or often a couple, comes in to cover all the particulars of a future cremation. I spend time walking around the building with elderly people who ask me about their corporal fate. "What will happen to me?" they say. "What can I expect?"

And so I tell them:

Near the end of your cremation, when your blood and eyeballs, skin and muscle, organ meat and marrow have vaporized up the smokestack into the wind above this river-hugging corridor populated by machine shops and body shops, an adult bookstore called Fantasy Island with a cartoon palm tree on its sign, a split-unit building housing Mister Chubby's take-out sandwich shop and ABC bail bonds, and several gravel lots full of the mammoth white bodies of shrink-wrapped pleasure boats on blocks, the cremationist will knock free your final piece of wet matter.

Most nights near six o'clock, but especially tonight with a pair of Sixers tickets folded in his wallet, your cremationist will slide a body into each of the three cremation machines, set the timers for three hours, and wait fifteen minutes to make sure each cremation has safely achieved a temperature of 1850 degrees. Then he'll leave for the night and his co-worker will process your cremated remains in the morning. But, like you've said, you're being buried in the Poconos first thing in the morning. So he depresses a green button on the front panel of the cremation machine—the boss has instructed the men never to call it an oven—engaging hydraulics that raise its four-inch-thick door high enough for a look, but not so high that the chamber loses temperature drastically. The machine, covered in silver tread plate, stands roughly the size of a small moving truck. Its steel frame conceals a brick hearth not much different from an artisan pizza oven. Bending to peer in, he burps the chicken-parm sandwich from Mister Chubby's he ate for lunch, tastes the three cans of Diet Dr Pepper slugged since, the half dozen Goldenberg's Peanut Chews sucked while typing your unique five-digit cremation number onto paperwork. He has seen you ablaze for two hours now. To speed your immolation he has over these hours regularly cracked the door and shattered you with an eight-foot steel rod that looks like a garden hoe. He tugs your remaining fleshy parts under the flame that jets from a hole in the ceiling of the brick chamber down to the level of what had been your chest. Despite previous blows, your skull has maintained its form even at nearly two thousand degrees. Late in your cremation, though, your cranial sutures will fail like the rest of your connective tissue.

He puts his hands inside his favorite royal blue welder's gloves, cowhide, with a soft cotton lining, and reaches for the rod again. His boss taught him to wear a heat-resistant face shield, too, whenever tending to an active cremation—one for each of the five employees hangs on the wall—but he has never seen his boss or any of the other men wear one and he hasn't worn one since his first week. He adapted to the heat right away. He never thinks about it. He has worked here eight years now and cremated more than eight thousand people. Now you.

All your watery parts are gone but one. The orange flames that cloaked your body, fueled by your fat, have gone. The only fire left is what the machine makes, and so he swings the pole to jab, just once, your desiccated skull, shivering it, freeing its sizzling content. Eight thousand times this annihilation has released under the cremationist's breastbone a single rising soda bubble of pleasure.

Each piece of you that lies on this machine's concrete floor has been wasted by fire and, though it survived longest, your brain has not been spared. A dull blade of flat metal has been driven through the roof of your skull by a man with Sixers tickets. Your brain has rolled from its housing like a Nerf basketball dipped in egg. It smells to the cremationist, a young man, a boy really, of thirty-one, like burnt hot dogs at a tailgate party. When it has come to rest a foot from the shattered bits of your skull, he has pushed it deeper into the machine, under the flame. After deft flicks of the hoe to make for your brain a nest of your crushed rib cage, he has tapped the hoe down on it, breaking it into several pieces, increasing the surface area for flame to reach, hastening the process, because he's late to pick up his date and late for tip-off, and in a few minutes your brain will have disappeared up the smokestack. You will have no brain. And you will be as carefree as he.

The Acme was shuttered after it lost business to a new ShopRite on Aramingo Avenue. Part of the attraction of the ShopRite is its on-premises Bank of America branch. People on Orthodox who could walk to the Acme now had to bus or carpool the two miles to the ShopRite. That or use the grocery a mile away that hoped to lure poor Latinos with lard and Bimbo cakes and old cookies and fruit punch and no produce besides bananas. Almost a year after the Acme closed, three men robbed the Bank of America inside the ShopRite. The first officer who responded was shot in the face and killed. The men who committed the crime were killed by police.

Another day during this same time I drove up to my dad's house and was told by police to park a few blocks away. Three whole blocks covered in cop cars. When I saw my dad he said, "You didn't hear?" The night before two guys had robbed Pat's Café, the bar around the corner, the bar where my dad used to go for beers with other coaches at the rec center. The responding officer had his head blown off at the kitchen door by a guy waiting for him with a shotgun. A kid I'd played soccer with, Mike, sat at the bar with the other patrons, a gun held on them.

Around this same time I got a call that Lucas, my buddy who'd signed my cast, who'd sold me a car, had shot himself. His wife had threatened to leave him and take their daughters. As we stood in line inside St. Martin's waiting to pass his casket and hug his mom and sisters, a woman screamed outside the church. Murmurs of other voices filtered in. "Get her away. She can't be in here." Then more screaming.

Frankford's an angry druggie gun boy. Frankford's bleeding out. Gazz goes to every neighborhood in the city to fix freezers in pizza shops and bodegas, and one day he says, "To tell you the truth, Frankford's the scariest. I don't know what it is, but I go there with fear."

Before many more years pass, St. Joachim's church and school, and Northeast Catholic, my high school, are all closed. We are under siege, our way stations gone.

———————

Father:

Omar took a call from a funeral director about an incoming cremation case. When he was done he did something unusual and handed me the slip. Normally he'd just put it on the pile. "Look," he said. I read the deceased's name, saw that he was coming from one of our regular funeral home clients out in Chester County. Arriving in a wood casket. Leaving us in a companion urn that already contained his wife's cremated remains. Age: forty-two. A little young but not remarkable to us, since we cremated a few people in their forties every week.

"What?" I said.

"Look." His thumb tapped the line for date of death. He had written "May 1948."

He had died as a relatively young man, and his wife had lived more than a half century without him. When she died and was cremated, the couple's sons had decided to have their father exhumed and cremated so he could share an urn with their mother.

That afternoon a flatbed truck pulled into our parking lot with a concrete casket vault loaded on the back. Omar, Dave, and I went outside to see. I had cremated a few exhumed cases before, and the caskets had been a mess: the wood gone black and pulpy from water exposure, the stench of the body and the rotting wood unbearable. And those cases had each been buried only a few years.

The truck driver set the straps under the casket, hooked them to the winch. He pulled a lever, and slowly the casket rose from the vault. I was expecting the worst, something like a sixty-year-old box of kimchee. But the casket fairly gleamed, its pale pine finish intact. The bottom had begun to give, and what looked like hay fringed out at the corners. But the casket was fine, considering. And there was no odor really at all. Standing there, we took in only the usual smells of the parking lot: exhaust from passing traffic, a hint of the tangy Delaware, a note of coffee from the roasting plant a few miles down the river.

The casket was lowered onto a church truck, and we rolled it inside the garage. Once the flatbed driver left, I remember Dave said, "Well?" We agreed we wanted to see. Dave slowly opened the casket. It was probably the first time since my dad and I had picked up Carl in his mausoleum of an apartment that I was conscious on the job of how powerfully my heart was beating. I assumed we were about to see a skeleton. I thought of my dad's parents and how whatever this guy looked like was what they must look like now, after twenty years in the ground. What if he still had meat on his bones but rats had been in the casket and gnawed away his eyes, his cheeks?

Dave opened the casket lid. I remember saying, "Whoa." After fifty-seven years, the part in his hair remained. His houndstooth blazer: spotless. Necktie perfectly knotted. Folded hands resting on his sternum. A program from his funeral left neatly on his chest. His skin had taken on a slight green pallor, and it seemed the flesh under the skin had deteriorated: he was skin and bones. But mostly he could've passed as a freshly embalmed man of the new millennium. In almost all cases we would have closed the garage door before opening a casket, for privacy and propriety's sake. But this day closing it didn't occur to any of us. It felt like he belonged to the outdoors more than he ever could to our little building. Maybe, too, there was a sense of his deserving the sun.

Son:

Once or twice a week a funeral director would arrive carrying a large, glossy-finished paper bag with rope handles and sharp corners, the kind of bag a department store gives for carrying a sweater or jacket, a purchase of bulk. The babies the funeral directors brought us in these bags rarely had bulk. For every ten-pound newborn, I'd say we cremated ten fetuses and preemies. And aside from these, we very rarely cremated children at all. Maybe twenty times in nine years did I cremate a child between two and eighteen.

I never see the baby's face if I don't want to, and I can't remember ever wanting. I don't need to; it comes from the hospital wrapped in a blue absorbent pad with an ID card taped to the outside, or sometimes it comes taped up in a fleece blanket decorated with little pastel animal shapes.

Even though it's cleaned, cold, too small to generate much stink, and though I don't even have to see it, I hate the simple act of lifting the baby's body from the shopping bag into the pan it will be cremated in. I grimace as my fingertips, protected by plastic gloves and by the hospital wrapping, recognize its contours, the way most of its weight falls to whichever hand has the head. I don't like the weight of an entire person in my hands. It's something that never happens with adults. I lift them in stages, always using leverage. So I avoid handling babies whenever I can. I let one of the other guys do it. If I have to, I do it as fast as possible and, I notice one day, without breathing.

The baby burns in a tin pan the shape of a hatbox. In the cremation machine we set the pan directly under the main burner, the orange monster that rages down on an adult's torso. Because of the pan's high sides, I don't see the baby burning. When an hour under the flame is done, I pull out the pan, its contents white filigree, an abstract rendering in the shape of a sleeping baby. I leave the pan to cool behind the machine, out of sight of anyone like the mailman or another funeral director who might walk through the cremation floor.

When it can be touched, I hold the pan over the processing tray and with a three-inch paintbrush sweep out each wisp and pearl. With the heavy magnet doubling as a mortar, I spread out the tiny pile, some of the vertebrae as delicate as a flounder's. I scrape the magnet back and forth, firm, crush and slide, crush and slide, until the chunks give way to a thin film of tan powder. I tilt the tray to dump the remnants of the baby's body into a plastic bag, like any other set of cremated remains. But where an adult's cremation might render seven pounds and fill three-quarters of the clear bag, a baby's ounce fills just a corner. So it will fit its stick-of-butter-size urn, I cut away the bag's excess, heat-sealing what's left into a sturdy packet, like a rare spice, or a night's portion of a drug.

It's in the process of making arrangements that I notice a change. I'm back at a kitchen table, just like on Oakland Street, again made to sit with grief, but now I am the one leading the session. It is my competence that a grieving family needs more than anything else. This is the discovery I make in this year. That because I am a stranger, any more than a few comforting words are inappropriate. The comfort I provide will not come from niceties. The comfort I provide, the gift I can give, will come from doing my job. If the urn is properly engraved and polished, if all the grandchildren's names are spelled correctly in the death notice, if the veterans' cemetery is expecting the family's arrival, if the Social Security benefit comes through without issue, then I have succeeded. If any of these things causes the family hassle, then it will only compound their day's grief. After eight years, I now see that I am working for the living. For the first time I am engaging with families in grief, and for the first time I see how important the job has been all along. I start to see the dignity in doing the necessary. I wonder if this is what it means to be a man, to carry out responsibilities, to relish them, to see them as a way to protect others.

———

Go to the door. Two middle-aged women trying to see in, daughters of the deceased. "Hello." Lips pursed. Slight bow. Concierge of their grief. "Can I show you around before we sit down?" Lead them to the showroom. Urns are fondled. The shopping element of these arrangements seems to calm the grieving. "This one? This is a cloisonné urn. It also comes in a smaller keepsake size." *Cloisonné* means "little walls." "Those? Those are charms that we can fill with cremated remains. The teardrop's popular. And the heart. You can get them in either silver or gold. Would you like to see the chapel?" Walking. Sunshine through stained glass. "It seats up to seventy-five. It's nice, right? And we can arrange for a priest or minister, or you can. Whatever's more comfortable for you. And this next room—Let me just draw the blinds in here first." I get to the window before they see, in the foreground, a cardboard casket lined up in front of a cremation machine, in the back, Larry in the office biting a hard pretzel. "This is the family witnessing room. Behind the blinds is where the cremations happen. Some people, for peace of mind, want to witness the start of their loved one's cremation. Other people, that idea does not appeal to them. It's completely up to you."

This is how arrangements go. Presenting options. Staying low key. Seeming in charge of possibilities. Using the numbness to death that comes with the business as a tool for good.

———

Hmong Buddhists from a temple in Kensington come nearly every Saturday. Dave and Omar have Saturdays off, so I'm left in charge. A hundred people swamp the chapel, fifteen or twenty more in the narrow witnessing room. They bring grocery bags filled with sandwiches and cans of soda to make a day of it.

When the incense has been burned, after the prayers have been sung, Larry and I wheel the casket through the doorway onto the cremation floor. All the attendees follow and form a semicircle around the open mouth of the machine. Larry and I roll the casket into the hearth, which elicits wails from the crowd. When I lower the door and it finally thuds shut, the wailing grows. I turn to the funeral director and mouth the word "Okay," and he pats a boy on the back.

The boy, maybe twelve years old, dressed in an orange monk's robe, his head newly shaved, steps forward. It seems the eldest boy of the youngest generation is the one who must start the fire. He looks at me as he approaches. Trembly lips. I nod and raise my finger to the control panel and let it rest on the green button. His eyes say, "Don't make me do this." I nod in a way that I hope says, "You'll be okay." He takes a deep breath. He pushes the button. An awful metallic whine rises up, igniting screams from the gathered. The monks lead the mourners in chanting. The boy steps back, sobbing, buries his head in a woman's chest.

———

I started to get thank-you notes in the mail. With women I dated, I only ever believed my actions would come to bad. Everything was headed to pain when they sniffed out how absent I was. With families, I started to see that I could steer a situation the other way. I was helping them through a few of the worst days of their lives. The irony of course is that none of this was ending well for the families. They were going through the worst loss, and I was finding in it my salvation.

It was this small trickle of good feeling about myself, the hints at competence, that led me to apply to graduate school.

———

Insights came, stuff that had passed me by on the job the first time, before I'd gone to California. I saw how Omar and Dave's fighting was secondary to the point, that they got their work done, and it was good and helpful work. And it let me see the same was true for my parents. They didn't get along, they were passive and screwy in how they handled their falling-out, but the bigger point was that they raised two kids who were relatively thoughtful, decent, not actively involved in harming other people. I spent so much time looking for reasons to tear them down, but the truth was that they'd succeeded at raising their kids, without the benefit of much money, without the benefit of having any idea of how to communicate. They were both kind, wary of conflict, sensitive—the worst people for working out trouble. It was their fate to be different from each other in ways they couldn't reconcile.

———

My mother's father has a heart attack on Thanksgiving, a few days before I turn thirty. He's eighty-seven. It feels likely from the beginning that he'll die in the hospital this winter. One night we go back to Mom's house for a late dinner after visiting hours. She's inching up on sixty. Her hair's gray, but she's naturally tanned and somehow getting prettier with age. She carries herself—her smile, her understated jewelry, her tasteful clothes—like someone with money, with ease in her life. Of course she's not. She runs a Catholic school in the city where she's in charge of a few hundred kids, a few dozen employees, and the financial health of the institution. She seems equal parts drained and charged by having the welfare of so many people on her back. For most of the school year she leaves her house in the dark and returns in the dark. She makes less than a mailman, but she wouldn't change it. She's become the ideal version of herself, a person whose energies are almost completely devoted to others, without my dad around.

After we eat she goes to bed. I have no one to go home to so I stay and watch the end of the Sixers game. They suck—back in the generation-long rut where the best they can do is make the last playoff seed, but still we watch, Gazz and Wilbur and I. Still we pay for tickets to justify hanging out.

Before I leave I check on her. Her bedroom door's left open, like always, like Oakland Street. The TV's on but her eyes are closed, a thin black void between her lips, the muscles in her face given over to serenity. In her face I see my grandfather, I see his deathbed, and I see hers, too. Some stooge in a suit will untuck that bottom sheet one night and be gone with her in thirty seconds. If he's like me, he'll stop at Arby's on the way back to the funeral home. A pulse of foreboding contracts my middle. I exhale. Her eyes open. "Are you going?" she says. She's fine. Years, decades before her death. *Live, Son.* I say, "Yeah, I'm going."

7

Dad asked me to lunch a few days before Christmas 2007, a few weeks short of his sixtieth birthday. But even with his great wavy hair all white now, even with the wrinkles framing his eyes and his hands' creeping liver spots, he looked better than his age. We walked around downtown, got lunch, went into the Bourse. He bought chocolates for his girlfriend. We walked through the Curtis Building and checked out the Tiffany mosaic there. When we were back near my apartment, I walked him to his car, and as he was saying good-bye he said, "I think we're going to get married."

A body blow. I took a second while he scanned my face. "Really?" I said to him. I wanted to pretend to be happy for him, but I failed instantly. I felt like a brat, but I couldn't help it.

"Yeah. We're really happy, buddy."

I wanted to let him have it, but the only words I could manage were "Do you have to do this at Christmas? You know I'm going to be the one who has to tell Mom, right?"

He said, "I want you to know I really love her." For a moment I felt confused and maybe elated. Did he mean Mom? I felt this weird hope rise in me. Was he saying I could talk him into making a case for going back to Mom? "She's really good for me," he said, "and we want to get married."

It had been seventeen years since he'd lost his job at La Salle. I had just turned thirty-two. I was fourteen when he was fired. I'd become a man, sort of. I'd spent nearly fifteen years since high school scuffling. Working a job I didn't want. Taking ten years to finish college. Having consistently and sometimes stupendously failed with women. And here he was, not miserable but, it felt to us, the carrier of our misery. That was the one thing we had to get past. We had to say to ourselves and mean it: he is not the cause of our misery. That he was the only one of the four of us who was happy at this late date, galling as it was to admit, was only our fault. Mom, Theresa, and I were still stuck in the trauma of 1990, and he had crashed, burned, and reemerged. He had found a woman and was choosing a second chance at a family. It was like the universe was offering him a window back into the moment things turned sour for him. His girlfriend was forty-one, her son fourteen, the same ages my mother and I had been when he was fired. But because we had moved so little beyond that point, it felt like his coming marriage was a betrayal. Our guts told us he was leaving us for his new wife, when really he'd lived alone for five years before he even met her. How many more years would we let pass like this, still so vulnerable to someone who meant us no harm?

————

After Dad's news, a thought surfaced: my parents don't need me in town anymore. Dad had ended the gridlock. And maybe I was never needed as much as I thought. But the possibility of Mom and Dad getting back together was ending officially. Six weeks after he told me of his wedding plans I was accepted to school in North Carolina.

————

The thing I discovered in my late approach to growing up is the peace in realizing there is nothing special in the traumas that form us. Some children have parents die, some see siblings die, some commit murder, some see their parents split. This is to say nothing of what war does. We cherish the particulars of our past, these events that cause our pain, but the liberation comes when we start to see how every living person has gone through something that has changed him or her, and that becoming an adult is based on response. If there were ever a measure put on the value of a life, that's what it would weigh: response. How one responds to trouble. How quickly. With how much goodness. How much strength.

8

People have asked me, knowing I spent late nights at work alone in a building with maybe eight corpses in the holding room, three being actively burned, four whose bones needed pulverizing, one laid out embalmed in the chapel for the next morning's viewing, if I encountered ghosts there. I've always found it silly. What amount of vanity would compel a dead man to follow his body? Home is the place to look.

———

"I had a relationship with a student," my father said. It had taken me forever to ask him what happened at La Salle more than twenty years ago—I was already finished with grad school—and now he was on the phone revealing his secret the first time I'd dared broach it, like it wasn't a secret at all. "We had a romance," he said. His voice sounded like rare meat. "It wasn't even physical, but a real romance." And then he added, "A terrible mistake."

My father's first book wasn't published until three years after he was fired. Instead of announcing the start of a punchy career, it felt more like a requiem for so many kinds of promise. But the book's a gem, full of funny, honest poems written to the people he loved. On the whole we see a poet awash in appreciation for the gifts of family life. There's one though called "Summer of '88" that hints at trouble between my parents. (Maybe. Of course the speaker should never be taken for the poet himself.) But this one features a narrator up late at the kitchen table, reading, listening to the Chieftains on his Walkman. This is my father. The poem includes the line "poor dead Wallace Stevens, so married, so alone." It's maybe the only crack in the book's general angle of marital content.

I don't know what went on between my parents in the years before he was fired, but to think that he lost his reputation, his income, all his goodwill at home, for an unconsummated romance seems too much. How many men and women have romances outside their marriages that ignite and fizzle and no one's the wiser? If he hadn't been fired, who's to say his marriage wouldn't have healed in time? How much different would everything else have been?

———

After he told me, I brought up the time I'd met a teacher from La Salle who'd asked about "that woman." I reminded him that when he told Theresa and me the news he said he'd made students feel uncomfortable, said he'd touched their shoulders and knees. I told him I'd always been confused. So was it an affair with one woman or the harassment of students? Had he been accused of being a cheater or a predator? I had always wanted to know, but I had never wanted to learn.

He said that the administration had talked to "every female student I'd ever been nice to" and bullied them into saying he'd made them feel uncomfortable.

"And you didn't have tenure," I said. "They could fire you."

When we hung up I saw that the details, this far gone, didn't matter to me as much as I'd always thought. I was happy we'd talked, sad for the small, tender patch on which our lives had pivoted, sadder still for not having been brave enough to ask him sooner and relieve him of his silence.

———

When I was a toddler, a summer night would find my parents—one on the sofa, one on the love seat—lounging in shorts and bare feet. Many nights they were watching the Phillies on TV or listening to the game on the radio while they read. When I was still of the age—say two or three or four—that it was more natural to be on the floor than in a chair, I liked to wrap myself on their bare legs. I remember the smell of my mother's legs—the soap and fresh sweat and something else sweet and unnameable—and their smooth feel, and I remember small pricks in my chin from the shaved hair on the soft curve of her knee. I would press my nose to my young mother's calf and breathe in its scent. I would touch her toes with my fingers. Smell her ankles. Trace the arches of her feet. If I'm nearly three in this remembrance, she is twenty-nine. She can only bear so much of this hanging on, and if I lick her foot she jumps, and the game is over.

My father's legs are covered in black hairs the shape of a capital C. He has Cs on the tops of his big toes, too. Now I breathe in deeply the scent of his ankles. Sometimes I travel my tongue along the tops of his toes and he picks me up quick.

We have no wrinkles, no pains, no white hair. We have no brown spots on our arms. We are dark-haired, smooth, soft, strong, bright. We have a garden. We have Paul Simon and Billy Joel. We are not retired. Dad goes to La Salle to teach. Mom goes downtown to work as a secretary. I go to nursery school to learn.

My parents' smell is not like the honeysuckle in the yard. It is not like the chicken Mom cooks for dinner. It is not the smell of my Raggedy Andy doll's head. It is not my granny's cold cream. It is not like a rose in bloom or perfume or the hosed-down black soil beneath the tomato plants. It is, though, like my wrist and fingers and the back of my hand. When I'm put to bed, I have taken to licking these and breathing them in. It means my parents are here with me even as they watch TV downstairs without me.

Now I see myself as a young man, in a bedroom, breathing in the fragrance of a woman's neck. I'm kissing her, stroking her hair away from her face, sinking to glide my tongue along her thigh, trying, I see now, to propel myself back to the living room floor and to my parents' bare legs, to kiss myself back to their toes, their gentle fingers on my head, their low voices. Back inside their arms. Back to sleep on their laps. Back to their black hair. Back to pulling dandelions in the garden in the sun while tea bags steep in the jar of water on the low brick wall. Back to my arms around their necks. Back to before my sister came. Back to only me and only them, back to when they were indistinguishable in their love for me so as to be one Momand-Dad, back to the freshness of their bodies, the freshness of their breath in my ear, the freshness of their holding me, kissing me, the freshness of their saying my name and protecting me. It's okay. It's okay, buddy. You're okay. Quiet now. Quiet. It's okay. I'm here. I'm here. *I'm here*.

About the Author

Andrew Meredith has been awarded fellowships from the Fine Arts Work Center in Provincetown and Yaddo. He received an MFA in fiction from UNC-Greensboro.

VESTAVIA HILLS
LIBRARY IN THE FOREST
1221 MONTGOMERY HWY.
VESTAVIA HILLS, AL 35216
205-978-0155